A JOHN CATT PUBLICATION

Knowledge Quiz: A Level

Maths

$$x_{n+1} = x_n - \frac{f(x_n)}{f'(x_n)}$$

Tom Bennison

First published 2020

by John Catt Educational Ltd,
15 Riduna Park, Station Road,
Melton, Woodbridge IP12 1QT

Tel: +44 (0) 1394 389850
Email: enquiries@johncatt.com
Website: www.johncatt.com

© 2020 Tom Bennison

All rights reserved.

No part of this publication may be reproduced, stored in a retrieval system, transmitted in any form or by any means, electronic, mechanical, photocopying, recording, or otherwise, without the prior permission of the publishers.

Opinions expressed in this publication are those of the contributors and are not necessarily those of the publishers or the editors. We cannot accept responsibility for any errors or omissions.

ISBN: 978 1 913 622 07 7

Set and designed by John Catt Educational Ltd

How to use this book

1	Start with Quiz 1. Use the answer key to memorise the knowledge.
2	If you see anything unfamiliar, make sure you look it up or ask your teacher about it.
3	When you're ready, complete the first quiz from memory.
4	Mark it using the answer key.
5	Record your score in the quiz tracker.
6	Leave it a few days, then try the same quiz again. We've rearranged the order of the questions on the quiz sheets to further challenge your knowledge retrieval.
7	Keep completing the same quiz every few days until you get full marks every time.
8	Move on to the next quiz and repeat steps 1–8.
9	Revisit previously mastered quizzes after a few weeks or months to check you still know the content.

Which quizzes should I complete?

This book is suitable for all A-level Maths students, irrespective of exam board. It contains quizzes on the key knowledge for each topic area, as well as some general mixed revision quizzes. This book should be used alongside plenty of past paper question practice to ensure you achieve to your highest potential.

Important!

This book will help you to memorise most of the knowledge that you need for A-level Maths. There are many other things you need to do to prepare for your exams – including lots and lots of practice. Memorising definitions and facts gives you the fundamental knowledge you need, and being able to **apply** that knowledge is the next challenge.

Contents

Quiz	Started?	Achieved 100%?	Revisited?
1. Proof			
2. Algebra			
3. Coordinate geometry			
4. Sequences and series			
5A. Trigonometry			
5B. Trigonometry			
6. Exponentials and logarithms			
7. Differentiation			
8. Integration			
9. Numerical methods			
10. Vectors			
11. Statistical sampling			
12. Data presentation and interpretation			
13. Probability			
14. Statistical distributions			
15. Statistical hypothesis testing			
16. Kinematics			
17. Forces and Newton's laws			
18. Moments			
Revision			
R1. Revision 1			
R2. Revision 2			
R3. Revision 3			
R4. Revision 4			
R5. Revision 5			

Quiz 1: Proof

ANSWER KEY

1.1	What is a direct proof?	A direct proof is where known (or previously proved) facts are used to build up a proof of a statement
1.2	What approach do you take to show that there are an infinite number of primes?	Proof by contradiction
1.3	What symbol is used to denote the set of rational numbers?	$\mathbb{Q}$
1.4	Describe proof by contradiction	In proof by contradiction, you assume the statement you are trying to prove is false and then show that this would lead to an impossibility (a contradiction)
1.5	What is meant by "$P \Rightarrow Q$"?	"P implies Q" or "if P then Q"
1.6	Is it true that $x^2 = 9 \Leftrightarrow x = 3$?	No. $x = 3 \Rightarrow x^2 = 9$ is true, but $x^2 = 9 \Rightarrow x = 3$ is not, since x could also be -3
1.7	When proving that $\sqrt{3}$ is irrational, what would be the first statement of the proof?	"Assume, for a contradiction, that $\sqrt{3}$ is rational"
1.8	What does $\{x : -3 < x < 5, x \in \mathbb{R}\}$ mean?	The set of values x in the reals that are less than 5 but greater than -3
1.9	For a direct proof involving odd numbers, how could you present a general odd number?	$2n + 1$ for integer n
1.10	What is a proof by exhaustion?	A proof where the result is split into a discrete number of cases and then each case is individually shown to be true
1.11	What is the meaning of the $\equiv$ symbol?	$\equiv$ is the identity symbol and means "identically equal". The expression on the left of $\equiv$ will always be equal to the expression on the right regardless of what values are substituted for the variables
1.12	To disprove a statement, what is it sufficient to do?	Find one counter-example to the statement

Quiz 1: Proof

TRACKER

Quiz	Date	Score
1		
2		
3		
4		
5		
6		

Got it? ☐

Quiz 1: Proof

1.1	What is a direct proof?	
1.2	What approach do you take to show that there are an infinite number of primes?	
1.3	What symbol is used to denote the set of rational numbers?	
1.4	Describe proof by contradiction	
1.5	What is meant by "$P \Rightarrow Q$"?	
1.6	Is it true that $x^2 = 9 \Leftrightarrow x = 3$?	
1.7	When proving that $\sqrt{3}$ is irrational, what would be the first statement of the proof?	
1.8	What does $\{x : -3 < x < 5, x \in \mathbb{R}\}$ mean?	
1.9	For a direct proof involving odd numbers, how could you present a general odd number?	
1.10	What is a proof by exhaustion?	
1.11	What is the meaning of the $\equiv$ symbol?	
1.12	To disprove a statement, what is it sufficient to do?	

Quiz 1: Proof

What symbol is used to denote the set of rational numbers?	
Is it true that $x^2 = 9 \Leftrightarrow x = 3$?	
For a direct proof involving odd numbers, how could you present a general odd number?	
To disprove a statement, what is it sufficient to do?	
What approach do you take to show that there are an infinite number of primes?	
Describe proof by contradiction	
What does $\{x : -3 < x < 5, x \in \mathbb{R}\}$ mean?	
What is a proof by exhaustion?	
What is a direct proof?	
What is meant by "$P \Rightarrow Q$"?	
When proving that $\sqrt{3}$ is irrational, what would be the first statement of the proof?	
What is the meaning of the $\equiv$ symbol?	

Quiz 1: Proof

What is a proof by exhaustion?	
What is a direct proof?	
What is meant by "$P \Rightarrow Q$"?	
Is it true that $x^2 = 9 \Leftrightarrow x = 3$?	
What approach do you take to show that there are an infinite number of primes?	
For a direct proof involving odd numbers, how could you present a general odd number?	
When proving that $\sqrt{3}$ is irrational, what would be the first statement of the proof?	
What is the meaning of the $\equiv$ symbol?	
What does $\{x : -3 < x < 5, x \in \mathbb{R}\}$ mean?	
To disprove a statement, what is it sufficient to do?	
What symbol is used to denote the set of rational numbers?	
Describe proof by contradiction	

Quiz 1: Proof

Is it true that $x^2 = 9 \Leftrightarrow x = 3$?	
To disprove a statement, what is it sufficient to do?	
What is a direct proof?	
What symbol is used to denote the set of rational numbers?	
When proving that $\sqrt{3}$ is irrational, what would be the first statement of the proof?	
What is meant by "$P \Rightarrow Q$"?	
What is the meaning of the $\equiv$ symbol?	
What does $\{x : -3 < x < 5, x \in \mathbb{R}\}$ mean?	
Describe proof by contradiction	
What is a proof by exhaustion?	
What approach do you take to show that there are an infinite number of primes?	
For a direct proof involving odd numbers, how could you present a general odd number?	

Quiz 1: Proof

What symbol is used to denote the set of rational numbers?	
Is it true that $x^2 = 9 \Leftrightarrow x = 3$?	
For a direct proof involving odd numbers, how could you present a general odd number?	
To disprove a statement, what is it sufficient to do?	
What approach do you take to show that there are an infinite number of primes?	
Describe proof by contradiction	
What does $\{x : -3 < x < 5, x \in \mathbb{R}\}$ mean?	
What is a proof by exhaustion?	
What is a direct proof?	
What is meant by "$P \Rightarrow Q$"?	
When proving that $\sqrt{3}$ is irrational, what would be the first statement of the proof?	
What is the meaning of the $\equiv$ symbol?	

Quiz 1: Proof

What is a proof by exhaustion?	
What is a direct proof?	
What is meant by "$P \Rightarrow Q$"?	
Is it true that $x^2 = 9 \Leftrightarrow x = 3$?	
What approach do you take to show that there are an infinite number of primes?	
For a direct proof involving odd numbers, how could you present a general odd number?	
When proving that $\sqrt{3}$ is irrational, what would be the first statement of the proof?	
What is the meaning of the $\equiv$ symbol?	
What does $\{x : -3 < x < 5, x \in \mathbb{R}\}$ mean?	
To disprove a statement, what is it sufficient to do?	
What symbol is used to denote the set of rational numbers?	
Describe proof by contradiction	

Quiz 2: Algebra

ANSWER KEY

2.1	What does $a^{\frac{1}{m}}$ equal?	$a^{\frac{1}{m}} = \sqrt[m]{a}$
2.2	Define the modulus $\|x\|$ of a number x	$\|x\| = \begin{cases} x & \text{if } x \geq 0 \\ -x & \text{if } x < 0 \end{cases}$
2.3	What would be the form of the partial fraction decomposition of $\dfrac{3x+2}{(x+1)(x+2)}$?	$\dfrac{A}{x+1} + \dfrac{B}{x+2}$
2.4	What is the discriminant of the quadratic $ax^2 + bx + c$?	$\Delta = b^2 - 4ac$
2.5	State the factor theorem	If $f\left(\dfrac{b}{a}\right) = 0$ then $(ax - b)$ is a factor of $f(x)$
2.6	Complete the surd equivalence $\sqrt{ab} =$	$\sqrt{ab} = \sqrt{a}\sqrt{b}$
2.7	How many possible intersection points are there between a circle and a parabola?	0, 1, 2, 3 or 4
2.8	What does "rationalising the denominator" mean?	Removing any surds from the denominator (bottom) of a fraction by multiplication by a suitable fraction
2.9	What effect does the transformation $y = f(x + a)$ have on the graph $y = f(x)$?	For $a > 0$, $y = f(x + a)$ is the graph of $y = f(x)$ but shifted a units to the left
2.10	Complete the square for the quadratic $ax^2 + bx + c$	$a\left(x + \dfrac{b}{2a}\right)^2 + \left(c - \dfrac{b^2}{4a}\right)$
2.11	How can you determine the nature of the roots of the quadratic equation $ax^2 + bx + c = 0$?	Use the discriminant. If $b^2 - 4ac < 0$ there are no real roots, if $b^2 - 4ac = 0$ there is a repeated root and if $b^2 - 4ac > 0$ there are 2 distinct real roots
2.12	If the coefficient of x^3 in a cubic is positive, describe what happens, as x is either very positive or very negative	If x is very positive then $f(x)$ is positive. If x is very negative then $f(x)$ is negative. Sometimes described as "bottom left to top right"

Quiz 2: Algebra

TRACKER

Quiz	Date	Score
1		
2		
3		
4		
5		
6		

Got it? ☐

Quiz 2: Algebra

2.1	What does $a^{\frac{1}{m}}$ equal?	
2.2	Define the modulus $|x|$ of a number x	
2.3	What would be the form of the partial fraction decomposition of $\dfrac{3x+2}{(x+1)(x+2)}$?	
2.4	What is the discriminant of the quadratic $ax^2 + bx + c$?	
2.5	State the factor theorem	
2.6	Complete the surd equivalence $\sqrt{ab}$ =	
2.7	How many possible intersection points are there between a circle and a parabola?	
2.8	What does "rationalising the denominator" mean?	
2.9	What effect does the transformation $y = f(x + a)$ have on the graph $y = f(x)$?	
2.10	Complete the square for the quadratic $ax^2 + bx + c$	
2.11	How can you determine the nature of the roots of the quadratic equation $ax^2 + bx + c = 0$?	
2.12	If the coefficient of x^3 in a cubic is positive, describe what happens, as x is either very positive or very negative	

Quiz 2: Algebra

What would be the form of the partial fraction decomposition of $\dfrac{3x+2}{(x+1)(x+2)}$?	
Complete the surd equivalence $\sqrt{ab} =$	
What effect does the transformation $y = f(x + a)$ have on the graph $y = f(x)$?	
If the coefficient of x^3 in a cubic is positive, describe what happens, as x is either very positive or very negative	
Define the modulus $|x|$ of a number x	
What is the discriminant of the quadratic $ax^2 + bx + c$?	
What does "rationalising the denominator" mean?	
Complete the square for the quadratic $ax^2 + bx + c$	
What does $a^{\frac{1}{m}}$ equal?	
State the factor theorem	
How many possible intersection points are there between a circle and a parabola?	
How can you determine the nature of the roots of the quadratic equation $ax^2 + bx + c = 0$?	

Quiz 2: Algebra

Complete the square for the quadratic $ax^2 + bx + c$	
What does $a^{\frac{1}{m}}$ equal?	
State the factor theorem	
Complete the surd equivalence $\sqrt{ab} =$	
Define the modulus $|x|$ of a number x	
What effect does the transformation $y = f(x + a)$ have on the graph $y = f(x)$?	
How many possible intersection points are there between a circle and a parabola?	
How can you determine the nature of the roots of the quadratic equation $ax^2 + bx + c = 0$?	
What does "rationalising the denominator" mean?	
If the coefficient of x^3 in a cubic is positive, describe what happens, as x is either very positive or very negative	
What would be the form of the partial fraction decomposition of $\dfrac{3x + 2}{(x + 1)(x + 2)}$?	
What is the discriminant of the quadratic $ax^2 + bx + c$?	

Quiz 2: Algebra

Complete the surd equivalence $\sqrt{ab}$ =	
If the coefficient of x^3 in a cubic is positive, describe what happens, as x is either very positive or very negative	
What does $a^{\frac{1}{m}}$ equal?	
What would be the form of the partial fraction decomposition of $\dfrac{3x+2}{(x+1)(x+2)}$?	
How many possible intersection points are there between a circle and a parabola?	
State the factor theorem	
How can you determine the nature of the roots of the quadratic equation $ax^2 + bx + c = 0$?	
What does "rationalising the denominator" mean?	
What is the discriminant of the quadratic $ax^2 + bx + c$?	
Complete the square for the quadratic $ax^2 + bx + c$	
Define the modulus $|x|$ of a number x	
What effect does the transformation $y = f(x + a)$ have on the graph $y = f(x)$?	

Quiz 2: Algebra

What would be the form of the partial fraction decomposition of $\dfrac{3x + 2}{(x + 1)(x + 2)}$?	
Complete the surd equivalence $\sqrt{ab} =$	
What effect does the transformation $y = f(x + a)$ have on the graph $y = f(x)$?	
If the coefficient of x^3 in a cubic is positive, describe what happens, as x is either very positive or very negative	
Define the modulus $|x|$ of a number x	
What is the discriminant of the quadratic $ax^2 + bx + c$?	
What does "rationalising the denominator" mean?	
Complete the square for the quadratic $ax^2 + bx + c$	
What does $a^{\frac{1}{m}}$ equal?	
State the factor theorem	
How many possible intersection points are there between a circle and a parabola?	
How can you determine the nature of the roots of the quadratic equation $ax^2 + bx + c = 0$?	

Quiz 2: Algebra

Complete the square for the quadratic $ax^2 + bx + c$	
What does $a^{\frac{1}{m}}$ equal?	
State the factor theorem	
Complete the surd equivalence $\sqrt{ab}$ =	
Define the modulus $\|x\|$ of a number x	
What effect does the transformation $y = f(x + a)$ have on the graph $y = f(x)$?	
How many possible intersection points are there between a circle and a parabola?	
How can you determine the nature of the roots of the quadratic equation $ax^2 + bx + c = 0$?	
What does "rationalising the denominator" mean?	
If the coefficient of x^3 in a cubic is positive, describe what happens, as x is either very positive or very negative	
What would be the form of the partial fraction decomposition of $\dfrac{3x + 2}{(x + 1)(x + 2)}$?	
What is the discriminant of the quadratic $ax^2 + bx + c$?	

Quiz 3: Coordinate geometry

ANSWER KEY

3.1	What is the equation of the line passing through (x_1, y_1) with gradient m?	$y - y_1 = m(x - x_1)$
3.2	What is the centre of the circle $(x - a)^2 + (y - b)^2 = r^2$?	(a, b)
3.3	What are the parametric equations of a circle?	The conventional form is $x = r\cos(\theta)$, $y = r\sin(\theta)$, however vice-versa would also work
3.4	If the gradient of line l_1 is m and line l_2 is perpendicular to l_1, what is the gradient of l_2?	$-\dfrac{1}{m}$
3.5	At what angle does the tangent to a circle meet the radius of the circle?	90°
3.6	A curve, C, given parametrically as $(x(t), y(t))$ intersects the line $y = mx + c$. How do you find the points of intersection?	Substitute the expressions $x(t)$ and $y(t)$ into the line $y = mx + c$ to find the value of t at the intersection points. Use this to find the coordinates of intersection
3.7	How do you find the midpoint of the points $A(x_A, y_A)$ and $B(x_B, y_B)$?	$\left(\dfrac{x_A + x_B}{2}, \dfrac{y_A + y_B}{2}\right)$
3.8	What is the gradient of a straight line given in the form $ax + by + c = 0$?	$-\dfrac{a}{b}$
3.9	How do you convert from the parametric form of a curve to the cartesian form?	If they contain trigonometric functions, try to use a trigonometric identity. If they don't, rearrange one of them so that the parameter is the subject and substitute in the others
3.10	How would you find the centre and radius of a circle given in the form $ax^2 + bx + cy^2 + dy + e = 0$?	Complete the square in x, complete the square in y and rearrange to the form $(x - m)^2 + (y - n)^2 = r^2$
3.11	Draw the circle theorem depicting "the angle in a semicircle is a right angle"	*(diagram of a circle with an inscribed right triangle on a diameter, right angle labelled C)*
3.12	How do you find the distance between the points $A(x_A, y_A)$ and $B(x_B, y_B)$?	Use Pythagoras' Theorem: $\|AB\| = \sqrt{(x_B - x_A)^2 + (y_B - y_A)^2}$

Quiz 3: Coordinate geometry

TRACKER

Quiz	Date	Score
1		
2		
3		
4		
5		
6		

Got it? ☐

Quiz 3: Coordinate geometry

3.1	What is the equation of the line passing through (x_1, y_1) with gradient m?	
3.2	What is the centre of the circle $(x - a)^2 + (y - b)^2 = r^2$?	
3.3	What are the parametric equations of a circle?	
3.4	If the gradient of line l_1 is m and line l_2 is perpendicular to l_1, what is the gradient of l_2?	
3.5	At what angle does the tangent to a circle meet the radius of the circle?	
3.6	A curve, C, given parametrically as $(x(t), y(t))$ intersects the line $y = mx + c$. How do you find the points of intersection?	
3.7	How do you find the midpoint of the points $A(x_A, y_A)$ and $B(x_B, y_B)$?	
3.8	What is the gradient of a straight line given in the form $ax + by + c = 0$?	
3.9	How do you convert from the parametric form of a curve to the cartesian form?	
3.10	How would you find the centre and radius of a circle given in the form $ax^2 + bx + cy^2 + dy + e = 0$?	
3.11	Draw the circle theorem depicting "the angle in a semicircle is a right angle"	
3.12	How do you find the distance between the points $A(x_A, y_A)$ and $B(x_B, y_B)$?	

Quiz 3: Coordinate geometry

What are the parametric equations of a circle?	
A curve, C, given parametrically as $(x(t), y(t))$ intersects the line $y = mx + c$. How do you find the points of intersection?	
How do you convert from the parametric form of a curve to the cartesian form?	
How do you find the distance between the points $A(x_A, y_A)$ and $B(x_B, y_B)$?	
What is the centre of the circle $(x - a)^2 + (y - b)^2 = r^2$?	
If the gradient of line l_1 is m and line l_2 is perpendicular to l_1, what is the gradient of l_2?	
What is the gradient of a straight line given in the form $ax + by + c = 0$?	
How would you find the centre and radius of a circle given in the form $ax^2 + bx + cy^2 + dy + e = 0$?	
What is the equation of the line passing through (x_1, y_1) with gradient m?	
At what angle does the tangent to a circle meet the radius of the circle?	
How do you find the midpoint of the points $A(x_A, y_A)$ and $B(x_B, y_B)$?	
Draw the circle theorem depicting "the angle in a semicircle is a right angle"	

Quiz 3: Coordinate geometry

How would you find the centre and radius of a circle given in the form $ax^2 + bx + cy^2 + dy + e = 0$?	
What is the equation of the line passing through (x_1, y_1) with gradient m?	
At what angle does the tangent to a circle meet the radius of the circle?	
A curve, C, given parametrically as $(x(t), y(t))$ intersects the line $y = mx + c$. How do you find the points of intersection?	
What is the centre of the circle $(x - a)^2 + (y - b)^2 = r^2$?	
How do you convert from the parametric form of a curve to the cartesian form?	
How do you find the midpoint of the points $A(x_A, y_A)$ and $B(x_B, y_B)$?	
Draw the circle theorem depicting "the angle in a semicircle is a right angle"	
What is the gradient of a straight line given in the form $ax + by + c = 0$?	
How do you find the distance between the points $A(x_A, y_A)$ and $B(x_B, y_B)$?	
What are the parametric equations of a circle?	
If the gradient of line l_1 is m and line l_2 is perpendicular to l_1, what is the gradient of l_2?	

Quiz 3: Coordinate geometry

A curve, C, given parametrically as $(x(t), y(t))$ intersects the line $y = mx + c$. How do you find the points of intersection?	
How do you find the distance between the points $A(x_A, y_A)$ and $B(x_B, y_B)$?	
What is the equation of the line passing through (x_1, y_1) with gradient m?	
What are the parametric equations of a circle?	
How do you find the midpoint of the points $A(x_A, y_A)$ and $B(x_B, y_B)$?	
At what angle does the tangent to a circle meet the radius of the circle?	
Draw the circle theorem depicting "the angle in a semicircle is a right angle"	
What is the gradient of a straight line given in the form $ax + by + c = 0$?	
If the gradient of line l_1 is m and line l_2 is perpendicular to l_1, what is the gradient of l_2?	
How would you find the centre and radius of a circle given in the form $ax^2 + bx + cy^2 + dy + e = 0$?	
What is the centre of the circle $(x - a)^2 + (y - b)^2 = r^2$?	
How do you convert from the parametric form of a curve to the cartesian form?	

Quiz 3: Coordinate geometry

What are the parametric equations of a circle?	
A curve, C, given parametrically as $(x(t), y(t))$ intersects the line $y = mx + c$. How do you find the points of intersection?	
How do you convert from the parametric form of a curve to the cartesian form?	
How do you find the distance between the points $A(x_A, y_A)$ and $B(x_B, y_B)$?	
What is the centre of the circle $(x - a)^2 + (y - b)^2 = r^2$?	
If the gradient of line l_1 is m and line l_2 is perpendicular to l_1, what is the gradient of l_2?	
What is the gradient of a straight line given in the form $ax + by + c = 0$?	
How would you find the centre and radius of a circle given in the form $ax^2 + bx + cy^2 + dy + e = 0$?	
What is the equation of the line passing through (x_1, y_1) with gradient m?	
At what angle does the tangent to a circle meet the radius of the circle?	
How do you find the midpoint of the points $A(x_A, y_A)$ and $B(x_B, y_B)$?	
Draw the circle theorem depicting "the angle in a semicircle is a right angle"	

Quiz 3: Coordinate geometry

How would you find the centre and radius of a circle given in the form $ax^2 + bx + cy^2 + dy + e = 0$?	
What is the equation of the line passing through (x_1, y_1) with gradient m?	
At what angle does the tangent to a circle meet the radius of the circle?	
A curve, C, given parametrically as $(x(t), y(t))$ intersects the line $y = mx + c$. How do you find the points of intersection?	
What is the centre of the circle $(x - a)^2 + (y - b)^2 = r^2$?	
How do you convert from the parametric form of a curve to the cartesian form?	
How do you find the midpoint of the points $A(x_A, y_A)$ and $B(x_B, y_B)$?	
Draw the circle theorem depicting "the angle in a semicircle is a right angle"	
What is the gradient of a straight line given in the form $ax + by + c = 0$?	
How do you find the distance between the points $A(x_A, y_A)$ and $B(x_B, y_B)$?	
What are the parametric equations of a circle?	
If the gradient of line l_1 is m and line l_2 is perpendicular to l_1, what is the gradient of l_2?	

Quiz 4: Sequences and series

ANSWER KEY

4.1	When is a sequence $\{a_n\}$ increasing?	$\{a_n\}$ is increasing if $a_{n+1} > a_n$ for all n
4.2	What is the sum of the first n terms of an arithmetic series?	$S_n = \dfrac{n}{2}[2a + (n-1)d]$ where a is the first term and d is the common difference
4.3	For the expansion of $(a + bx)^n$, with n either a fraction or negative integer, for what values of x is the expansion valid?	$\left|\dfrac{bx}{a}\right| < 1$ or $\|x\| < \left|\dfrac{a}{b}\right|$
4.4	For positive integer n, when is the expansion $(a + bx)^n$ valid?	For all values of x
4.5	Evaluate $S = \sum\limits_{r=1}^{5}(2r+2)$	40
4.6	What is a geometric progression?	A sequence where the next term is obtained by multiplying the previous term by a constant value, the common ratio
4.7	State the binomial theorem for $n \in \mathbb{N}$	$(a+bx)^n = \sum\limits_{r=0}^{n}\binom{n}{r}a^{n-r}b^r x^r$
4.8	How would you find the binomial expansion of $f(x) = \dfrac{2x-1}{(x+2)(x-3)}$?	First split $f(x) = \dfrac{2x-1}{(x+2)(x-3)}$ into partial fractions and then expand each part using the binomial expansion
4.9	What does it mean to say a series is "divergent"?	A series is divergent if as $n \to \infty$, $\sum\limits_{i=1}^{n} a_i \to \infty$
4.10	What is a periodic sequence?	A periodic sequence is one where the terms repeat in a cycle. The length of one cycle is known as the order of the sequence
4.11	Define $\binom{n}{r}$	$\binom{n}{r} = \dfrac{n!}{r!(n-r)!}$
4.12	What is the sum of the first n terms of a geometric series?	$S_n = \dfrac{a(1-r^n)}{1-r}$ where a is the first term, r is the common ratio

Quiz 4: Sequences and series

TRACKER

Quiz	Date	Score
1		
2		
3		
4		
5		
6		

Got it? ☐

Quiz 4: Sequences and series

4.1	When is a sequence $\{a_n\}$ increasing?	
4.2	What is the sum of the first n terms of an arithmetic series?	
4.3	For the expansion of $(a + bx)^n$, with n either a fraction or negative integer, for what values of x is the expansion valid?	
4.4	For positive integer n, when is the expansion $(a + bx)^n$ valid?	
4.5	Evaluate $S = \sum_{r=1}^{5} (2r + 2)$	
4.6	What is a geometric progression?	
4.7	State the binomial theorem for $n \in \mathbb{N}$	
4.8	How would you find the binomial expansion of $f(x) = \dfrac{2x - 1}{(x + 2)(x - 3)}$?	
4.9	What does it mean to say a series is "divergent"?	
4.10	What is a periodic sequence?	
4.11	Define $\binom{n}{r}$	
4.12	What is the sum of the first n terms of a geometric series?	

Quiz 4: Sequences and series

For the expansion of $(a + bx)^n$, with n either a fraction or negative integer, for what values of x is the expansion valid?	
What is a geometric progression?	
What does it mean to say a series is "divergent"?	
What is the sum of the first n terms of a geometric series?	
What is the sum of the first n terms of an arithmetic series?	
For positive integer n, when is the expansion $(a + bx)^n$ valid?	
How would you find the binomial expansion of $f(x) = \dfrac{2x - 1}{(x + 2)(x - 3)}$?	
What is a periodic sequence?	
When is a sequence $\{a_n\}$ increasing?	
Evaluate $S = \sum\limits_{r=1}^{5} (2r + 2)$	
State the binomial theorem for $n \in \mathbb{N}$	
Define $\binom{n}{r}$	

Quiz 4: Sequences and series

What is a periodic sequence?	
When is a sequence $\{a_n\}$ increasing?	
Evaluate $S = \sum_{r=1}^{5} (2r + 2)$	
What is a geometric progression?	
What is the sum of the first n terms of an arithmetic series?	
What does it mean to say a series is "divergent"?	
State the binomial theorem for $n \in \mathbb{N}$	
Define $\binom{n}{r}$	
How would you find the binomial expansion of $f(x) = \dfrac{2x - 1}{(x + 2)(x - 3)}$?	
What is the sum of the first n terms of a geometric series?	
For the expansion of $(a + bx)^n$, with n either a fraction or negative integer, for what values of x is the expansion valid?	
For positive integer n, when is the expansion $(a + bx)^n$ valid?	

Quiz 4: Sequences and series

What is a geometric progression?	
What is the sum of the first n terms of a geometric series?	
When is a sequence $\{a_n\}$ increasing?	
For the expansion of $(a + bx)^n$, with n either a fraction or negative integer, for what values of x is the expansion valid?	
State the binomial theorem for $n \in \mathbb{N}$	
Evaluate $S = \sum_{r=1}^{5}(2r + 2)$	
Define $\binom{n}{r}$	
How would you find the binomial expansion of $f(x) = \dfrac{2x - 1}{(x + 2)(x - 3)}$?	
For positive integer n, when is the expansion $(a + bx)^n$ valid?	
What is a periodic sequence?	
What is the sum of the first n terms of an arithmetic series?	
What does it mean to say a series is "divergent"?	

Quiz 4: Sequences and series

For the expansion of $(a + bx)^n$, with n either a fraction or negative integer, for what values of x is the expansion valid?	
What is a geometric progression?	
What does it mean to say a series is "divergent"?	
What is the sum of the first n terms of a geometric series?	
What is the sum of the first n terms of an arithmetic series?	
For positive integer n, when is the expansion $(a + bx)^n$ valid?	
How would you find the binomial expansion of $f(x) = \dfrac{2x - 1}{(x + 2)(x - 3)}$?	
What is a periodic sequence?	
When is a sequence $\{a_n\}$ increasing?	
Evaluate $S = \displaystyle\sum_{r=1}^{5} (2r + 2)$	
State the binomial theorem for $n \in \mathbb{N}$	
Define $\dbinom{n}{r}$	

Quiz 4: Sequences and series

What is a periodic sequence?	
When is a sequence $\{a_n\}$ increasing?	
Evaluate $S = \sum_{r=1}^{5} (2r + 2)$	
What is a geometric progression?	
What is the sum of the first n terms of an arithmetic series?	
What does it mean to say a series is "divergent"?	
State the binomial theorem for $n \in \mathbb{N}$	
Define $\binom{n}{r}$	
How would you find the binomial expansion of $f(x) = \dfrac{2x - 1}{(x + 2)(x - 3)}$?	
What is the sum of the first n terms of a geometric series?	
For the expansion of $(a + bx)^n$, with n either a fraction or negative integer, for what values of x is the expansion valid?	
For positive integer n, when is the expansion $(a + bx)^n$ valid?	

Quiz 5A: Trigonometry

ANSWER KEY

5A.1	How do you convert from radians to degrees?	Divide by π and multiply by 180
5A.2	State the small-angle approximations for $\sin(\theta)$, $\cos(\theta)$ and $\tan(\theta)$	$\sin(\theta) \approx \theta$, $\cos(\theta) \approx 1 - \frac{1}{2}\theta^2$ and $\tan(\theta) \approx \theta$
5A.3	State the sine rule	$\frac{a}{\sin(A)} = \frac{b}{\sin(B)} = \frac{c}{\sin(C)}$
5A.4	Complete the trigonometric identity $\tan(2x) \equiv$	$\tan(2x) = \frac{2\tan(x)}{1 - \tan^2(x)}$
5A.5	State the formula for the area of a sector with radius r and angle θ, measured in radians	$A = \frac{1}{2}r^2\theta$
5A.6	How is the factor formula $\cos(P) + \cos(Q) \equiv 2\cos\left(\frac{P+Q}{2}\right)\cos\left(\frac{P-Q}{2}\right)$ obtained?	Use the addition formulae for $\cos(P+Q)$ and $\cos(P-Q)$, add them together and rearrange
5A.7	Define $\tan(x)$	$\tan(x) = \frac{\sin(x)}{\cos(x)}$
5A.8	How would you put $A\sin(x) + B\cos(x)$ into the form $R\sin(x + a)$?	Use the addition formulae to write $A\sin(x) + B\cos(x) = \sin(x)\cos(a) + \cos(x)\sin(a)$ then $R = \sqrt{A^2 + B^2}$ and $a = \arctan\left(\frac{B}{A}\right)$
5A.9	When would you use the cosine rule?	When you know three sides of a triangle, or you know two sides and the angle between them
5A.10	What is $\text{cosec}(x)$?	$\text{cosec}(x) = \frac{1}{\sin(x)}$
5A.11	What are the three Pythagorean trigonometric identities?	$\cos^2(x) + \sin^2(x) \equiv 1$ $\sec^2(x) \equiv 1 + \tan^2(x)$ $\text{cosec}^2(x) \equiv 1 + \cot^2(x)$
5A.12	What is the period of $\tan(x)$ and when is it undefined?	The period of $\tan(x)$ is 180° and it is undefined at ±90°, ±270°, ±450°, ...

Quiz 5A: Trigonometry

TRACKER

Quiz	Date	Score
1		
2		
3		
4		
5		
6		

Got it? ☐

Quiz 5A: Trigonometry

5A.1	How do you convert from radians to degrees?	
5A.2	State the small-angle approximations for $\sin(\theta)$, $\cos(\theta)$ and $\tan(\theta)$	
5A.3	State the sine rule	
5A.4	Complete the trigonometric identity $\tan(2x) \equiv$	
5A.5	State the formula for the area of a sector with radius r and angle θ, measured in radians	
5A.6	How is the factor formula $\cos(P) + \cos(Q) \equiv 2\cos\left(\dfrac{P+Q}{2}\right)\cos\left(\dfrac{P-Q}{2}\right)$ obtained?	
5A.7	Define $\tan(x)$	
5A.8	How would you put $A\sin(x) + B\cos(x)$ into the form $R\sin(x+a)$?	
5A.9	When would you use the cosine rule?	
5A.10	What is $\operatorname{cosec}(x)$?	
5A.11	What are the three Pythagorean trigonometric identities?	
5A.12	What is the period of $\tan(x)$ and when is it undefined?	

Quiz 5A: Trigonometry

State the sine rule	
How is the factor formula $\cos(P) + \cos(Q) \equiv 2\cos\left(\frac{P+Q}{2}\right)\cos\left(\frac{P-Q}{2}\right)$ obtained?	
When would you use the cosine rule?	
What is the period of $\tan(x)$ and when is it undefined?	
State the small-angle approximations for $\sin(\theta)$, $\cos(\theta)$ and $\tan(\theta)$	
Complete the trigonometric identity $\tan(2x) \equiv$	
How would you put $A\sin(x) + B\cos(x)$ into the form $R\sin(x+a)$?	
What is $\operatorname{cosec}(x)$?	
How do you convert from radians to degrees?	
State the formula for the area of a sector with radius r and angle θ, measured in radians	
Define $\tan(x)$	
What are the three Pythagorean trigonometric identities?	

Quiz 5A: Trigonometry

What is $\text{cosec}(x)$?	
How do you convert from radians to degrees?	
State the formula for the area of a sector with radius r and angle θ, measured in radians	
How is the factor formula $\cos(P) + \cos(Q) \equiv 2\cos\left(\dfrac{P+Q}{2}\right)\cos\left(\dfrac{P-Q}{2}\right)$ obtained?	
State the small-angle approximations for $\sin(\theta)$, $\cos(\theta)$ and $\tan(\theta)$	
When would you use the cosine rule?	
Define $\tan(x)$	
What are the three Pythagorean trigonometric identities?	
How would you put $A\sin(x) + B\cos(x)$ into the form $R\sin(x+a)$?	
What is the period of $\tan(x)$ and when is it undefined?	
State the sine rule	
Complete the trigonometric identity $\tan(2x) \equiv$	

Quiz 5A: Trigonometry

How is the factor formula $\cos(P) + \cos(Q) \equiv 2\cos\left(\frac{P+Q}{2}\right)\cos\left(\frac{P-Q}{2}\right)$ obtained?	
What is the period of $\tan(x)$ and when is it undefined?	
How do you convert from radians to degrees?	
State the sine rule	
Define $\tan(x)$	
State the formula for the area of a sector with radius r and angle θ, measured in radians	
What are the three Pythagorean trigonometric identities?	
How would you put $A\sin(x) + B\cos(x)$ into the form $R\sin(x+a)$?	
Complete the trigonometric identity $\tan(2x) \equiv$	
What is $\operatorname{cosec}(x)$?	
State the small-angle approximations for $\sin(\theta)$, $\cos(\theta)$ and $\tan(\theta)$	
When would you use the cosine rule?	

Quiz 5A: Trigonometry

State the sine rule	
How is the factor formula $\cos(P) + \cos(Q) \equiv 2\cos\left(\dfrac{P+Q}{2}\right)\cos\left(\dfrac{P-Q}{2}\right)$ obtained?	
When would you use the cosine rule?	
What is the period of $\tan(x)$ and when is it undefined?	
State the small-angle approximations for $\sin(\theta)$, $\cos(\theta)$ and $\tan(\theta)$	
Complete the trigonometric identity $\tan(2x) \equiv$	
How would you put $A\sin(x) + B\cos(x)$ into the form $R\sin(x+a)$?	
What is $\operatorname{cosec}(x)$?	
How do you convert from radians to degrees?	
State the formula for the area of a sector with radius r and angle θ, measured in radians	
Define $\tan(x)$	
What are the three Pythagorean trigonometric identities?	

Quiz 5A: Trigonometry

What is $\operatorname{cosec}(x)$?	
How do you convert from radians to degrees?	
State the formula for the area of a sector with radius r and angle θ, measured in radians	
How is the factor formula $\cos(P) + \cos(Q) \equiv 2\cos\left(\dfrac{P+Q}{2}\right)\cos\left(\dfrac{P-Q}{2}\right)$ obtained?	
State the small-angle approximations for $\sin(\theta)$, $\cos(\theta)$ and $\tan(\theta)$	
When would you use the cosine rule?	
Define $\tan(x)$	
What are the three Pythagorean trigonometric identities?	
How would you put $A\sin(x) + B\cos(x)$ into the form $R\sin(x + a)$?	
What is the period of $\tan(x)$ and when is it undefined?	
State the sine rule	
Complete the trigonometric identity $\tan(2x) \equiv$	

Quiz 5B: Trigonometry

ANSWER KEY

5B.1	For an arc with radius r and angle θ (in radians) at the middle, how do you find the arc length?	$l = r\theta$
5B.2	What is the double angle formulae for the tangent function?	$\tan(2\theta) = \dfrac{2\tan(\theta)}{1 - \tan^2(\theta)}$
5B.3	What is the domain of $y = \arcsin(x)$?	$-1 \leq x \leq 1$
5B.4	Define $\sec(\theta)$	$\sec(\theta) = \dfrac{1}{\cos(\theta)}$
5B.5	How can you obtain the graph of $y = \arcsin(x)$ from the graph of $y = \sin(x)$?	Restrict the domain of $y = \sin(x)$ to $-\dfrac{\pi}{2} \leq x \leq \dfrac{\pi}{2}$ and then reflect in the line $y = x$
5B.6	What is the cosine rule for a triangle $A\,B\,C$?	$c^2 = a^2 + b^2 - 2ab\cos(C)$ where a, b and c are the sides opposite vertices A, B and C respectively
5B.7	What is $\sin(\pi - \theta)$ equal to?	$\sin(\theta)$
5B.8	What is the range of $y = \arctan(x)$?	$-\dfrac{\pi}{2} \leq \arctan(x) \leq \dfrac{\pi}{2}$
5B.9	Complete the identity $\sin(2A) \equiv$	$\sin(2A) = 2\sin(A)\cos(A)$
5B.10	What is the period for $y = \sec(x)$?	$360°$ or 2π radians
5B.11	What is the range of $y = \operatorname{cosec}(x)$?	$y \leq -1$ or $y \geq 1$
5B.12	Define $\cot(x)$	$\cot(x) = \dfrac{1}{\tan(x)}$

Quiz 5B: Trigonometry

TRACKER

Quiz	Date	Score
1		
2		
3		
4		
5		
6		

Got it? ☐

Quiz 5B: Trigonometry

5B.1	For an arc with radius r and angle θ (in radians) at the middle, how do you find the arc length?	
5B.2	What is the double angle formulae for the tangent function?	
5B.3	What is the domain of $y = \arcsin(x)$?	
5B.4	Define $\sec(\theta)$	
5B.5	How can you obtain the graph of $y = \arcsin(x)$ from the graph of $y = \sin(x)$?	
5B.6	What is the cosine rule for a triangle $A\ B\ C$?	
5B.7	What is $\sin(\pi - \theta)$ equal to?	
5B.8	What is the range of $y = \arctan(x)$?	
5B.9	Complete the identity $\sin(2A) \equiv$	
5B.10	What is the period for $y = \sec(x)$?	
5B.11	What is the range of $y = \operatorname{cosec}(x)$?	
5B.12	Define $\cot(x)$	

Quiz 5B: Trigonometry

What is the domain of $y = \arcsin(x)$?	
What is the cosine rule for a triangle $A\ B\ C$?	
Complete the identity $\sin(2A) \equiv$	
Define $\cot(x)$	
What is the double angle formulae for the tangent function?	
Define $\sec(\theta)$	
What is the range of $y = \arctan(x)$?	
What is the period for $y = \sec(x)$?	
For an arc with radius r and angle θ (in radians) at the middle, how do you find the arc length?	
How can you obtain the graph of $y = \arcsin(x)$ from the graph of $y = \sin(x)$?	
What is $\sin(\pi - \theta)$ equal to?	
What is the range of $y = \operatorname{cosec}(x)$?	

Quiz 5B: Trigonometry

What is the period for $y = \sec(x)$?	
For an arc with radius r and angle θ (in radians) at the middle, how do you find the arc length?	
How can you obtain the graph of $y = \arcsin(x)$ from the graph of $y = \sin(x)$?	
What is the cosine rule for a triangle $A\ B\ C$?	
What is the double angle formulae for the tangent function?	
Complete the identity $\sin(2A) \equiv$	
What is $\sin(\pi - \theta)$ equal to?	
What is the range of $y = \operatorname{cosec}(x)$?	
What is the range of $y = \arctan(x)$?	
Define $\cot(x)$	
What is the domain of $y = \arcsin(x)$?	
Define $\sec(\theta)$	

Quiz 5B: Trigonometry

What is the cosine rule for a triangle ABC?	
Define $\cot(x)$?	
For an arc with radius r and angle θ (in radians) at the middle, how do you find the arc length?	
What is the domain of $y = \arcsin(x)$?	
What is $\sin(\pi - \theta)$ equal to?	
How can you obtain the graph of $y = \arcsin(x)$ from the graph of $y = \sin(x)$?	
What is the range of $y = \text{cosec}(x)$?	
What is the range of $y = \arctan(x)$?	
Define $\sec(\theta)$	
What is the period for $y = \sec(x)$?	
What is the double angle formulae for the tangent function?	
Complete the identity $\sin(2A) \equiv$	

Quiz 5B: Trigonometry

What is the domain of $y = \arcsin(x)$?	
What is the cosine rule for a triangle ABC?	
Complete the identity $\sin(2A) \equiv$	
Define $\cot(x)$	
What is the double angle formulae for the tangent function?	
Define $\sec(\theta)$	
What is the range of $y = \arctan(x)$?	
What is the period for $y = \sec(x)$?	
For an arc with radius r and angle θ (in radians) at the middle, how do you find the arc length?	
How can you obtain the graph of $y = \arcsin(x)$ from the graph of $y = \sin(x)$?	
What is $\sin(\pi - \theta)$ equal to?	
What is the range of $y = \text{cosec}(x)$?	

Quiz 5B: Trigonometry

What is the period for $y = \sec(x)$?	
For an arc with radius r and angle θ (in radians) at the middle, how do you find the arc length?	
How can you obtain the graph of $y = \arcsin(x)$ from the graph of $y = \sin(x)$?	
What is the cosine rule for a triangle $A\ B\ C$?	
What is the double angle formulae for the tangent function?	
Complete the identity $\sin(2A) \equiv$	
What is $\sin(\pi - \theta)$ equal to?	
What is the range of $y = \operatorname{cosec}(x)$?	
What is the range of $y = \arctan(x)$?	
Define $\cot(x)$	
What is the domain of $y = \arcsin(x)$?	
Define $\sec(\theta)$	

Quiz 6: Exponentials and logarithms

ANSWER KEY

6.1	What is the derivative of e^{kx} with respect to x?	ke^{kx}
6.2	What is the horizontal asymptote for the function $f(x) = e^{2x} - 4$?	$y = -4$
6.3	How could you solve the equation $2^{3x} = 5$?	Take logarithms to the base 2 so that $3x = \log_2(5)$, hence $x = \dfrac{\log_2(5)}{3}$
6.4	What does $\log_a(b) = c$ mean?	$a^c = b$
6.5	What is the y-intercept of the function $y = e^x$?	1
6.6	What is the inverse function of e^x?	$\ln(x)$
6.7	Complete the logarithm law: $\log_a(x^n) =$	$\log_a(x^n) = n \log_a(x)$
6.8	How would you proceed to solve the equation $e^x + 6e^{-x} = 5$?	Multiply by e^x and rearrange to the quadratic $e^{2x} - 5e^x + 6 = 0$ and then solve. Then take logarithms to find the value(s) of x
6.9	Complete the logarithm law: $\log_a(x\,y) =$	$\log_a(x\,y) = \log_a(x) + \log_a(y)$
6.10	For the function $f(x) = 2e^{-2x}$, what happens as $x \to \infty$?	As $x \to \infty$, $f(x) \to 0$
6.11	For the radioactive decay $N = N_0 e^{-kt}$, how would you find the half life?	The half life is the time taken for the activity to be half of its initial value. Let $N = \dfrac{N_0}{2}$ and rearrange and solve
6.12	What is a limitation of using exponential growth to model a population of animals?	Exponential growth would lead to unbounded growth of the population. In reality, the growth is constrained by environmental factors

Quiz 6: Exponentials and logarithms

TRACKER

Quiz	Date	Score
1		
2		
3		
4		
5		
6		

Got it? ☐

Quiz 6: Exponentials and logarithms

6.1	What is the derivative of e^{kx} with respect to x?	
6.2	What is the horizontal asymptote for the function $f(x) = e^{2x} - 4$?	
6.3	How could you solve the equation $2^{3x} = 5$?	
6.4	What does $\log_a(b) = c$ mean?	
6.5	What is the y-intercept of the function $y = e^x$?	
6.6	What is the inverse function of e^x?	
6.7	Complete the logarithm law: $\log_a(x^n) =$	
6.8	How would you proceed to solve the equation $e^x + 6e^{-x} = 5$?	
6.9	Complete the logarithm law: $\log_a(x\,y) =$	
6.10	For the function $f(x) = 2e^{-2x}$, what happens as $x \to \infty$?	
6.11	For the radioactive decay $N = N_0 e^{-kt}$, how would you find the half life?	
6.12	What is a limitation of using exponential growth to model a population of animals?	

Quiz 6: Exponentials and logarithms

How could you solve the equation $2^{3x} = 5$?	
What is the inverse function of e^x?	
Complete the logarithm law: $\log_a(x\,y) =$	
What is a limitation of using exponential growth to model a population of animals?	
What is the horizontal asymptote for the function $f(x) = e^{2x} - 4$?	
What does $\log_a(b) = c$ mean?	
How would you proceed to solve the equation $e^x + 6e^{-x} = 5$?	
For the function $f(x) = 2e^{-2x}$, what happens as $x \to \infty$?	
What is the derivative of e^{kx} with respect to x?	
What is the y-intercept of the function $y = e^x$?	
Complete the logarithm law: $\log_a(x^n) =$	
For the radioactive decay $N = N_0 e^{-kt}$, how would you find the half life?	

Quiz 6: Exponentials and logarithms

For the function $f(x) = 2e^{-2x}$, what happens as $x \to \infty$?	
What is the derivative of e^{kx} with respect to x?	
What is the y- intercept of the function $y = e^x$?	
What is the inverse function of e^x?	
What is the horizontal asymptote for the function $f(x) = e^{2x} - 4$?	
Complete the logarithm law: $\log_a(x\,y) =$	
Complete the logarithm law: $\log_a(x^n) =$	
For the radioactive decay $N = N_0 e^{-kt}$, how would you find the half life?	
How would you proceed to solve the equation $e^x + 6e^{-x} = 5$?	
What is a limitation of using exponential growth to model a population of animals?	
How could you solve the equation $2^{3x} = 5$?	
What does $\log_a(b) = c$ mean?	

Quiz 6: Exponentials and logarithms

What is the inverse function of e^x?	
What is a limitation of using exponential growth to model a population of animals?	
What is the derivative of e^{kx} with respect to x?	
How could you solve the equation $2^{3x} = 5$?	
Complete the logarithm law: $\log_a(x^n) =$	
What is the y- intercept of the function $y = e^x$?	
For the radioactive decay $N = N_0 e^{-kt}$, how would you find the half life?	
How would you proceed to solve the equation $e^x + 6e^{-x} = 5$?	
What does $\log_a(b) = c$ mean?	
For the function $f(x) = 2e^{-2x}$, what happens as $x \to \infty$?	
What is the horizontal asymptote for the function $f(x) = e^{2x} - 4$?	
Complete the logarithm law: $\log_a(x\,y) =$	

Quiz 6: Exponentials and logarithms

How could you solve the equation $2^{3x} = 5$?	
What is the inverse function of e^x?	
Complete the logarithm law: $\log_a(x\,y) =$	
What is a limitation of using exponential growth to model a population of animals?	
What is the horizontal asymptote for the function $f(x) = e^{2x} - 4$?	
What does $\log_a(b) = c$ mean?	
How would you proceed to solve the equation $e^x + 6e^{-x} = 5$?	
For the function $f(x) = 2e^{-2x}$, what happens as $x \to \infty$?	
What is the derivative of e^{kx} with respect to x?	
What is the y-intercept of the function $y = e^x$?	
Complete the logarithm law: $\log_a(x^n) =$	
For the radioactive decay $N = N_0 e^{-kt}$, how would you find the half life?	

Quiz 6: Exponentials and logarithms

For the function $f(x) = 2e^{-2x}$, what happens as $x \to \infty$?	
What is the derivative of e^{kx} with respect to x?	
What is the y- intercept of the function $y = e^x$?	
What is the inverse function of e^x?	
What is the horizontal asymptote for the function $f(x) = e^{2x} - 4$?	
Complete the logarithm law: $\log_a(x\,y) =$	
Complete the logarithm law: $\log_a(x^n) =$	
For the radioactive decay $N = N_0 e^{-kt}$, how would you find the half life?	
How would you proceed to solve the equation $e^x + 6e^{-x} = 5$?	
What is a limitation of using exponential growth to model a population of animals?	
How could you solve the equation $2^{3x} = 5$?	
What does $\log_a(b) = c$ mean?	

Quiz 7: Differentiation

ANSWER KEY

7.1	What is the formal definition of the derivative of $f(x)$?	$f'(x) = \lim\limits_{h \to 0} \dfrac{f(x+h) - f(x)}{h}$
7.2	What is the derivative of $y = a^x$?	$\dfrac{dy}{dx} = a^x \ln(a)$
7.3	What is the condition for a point x_1 to be a point of inflection for the function $f(x)$?	$f''(x_1) = 0$
7.4	For a curve C defined parametrically (i.e. with $x = f(t)$, $y = g(t)$) how would you find $\dfrac{dy}{dx}$?	Use $\dfrac{dy}{dx} = \dfrac{dy}{dt} \div \dfrac{dx}{dt}$
7.5	State the product rule for the function $y(x) = u(x)v(x)$	$\dfrac{dy}{dx} = u\dfrac{dv}{dx} + v\dfrac{du}{dx}$
7.6	When is a function $f(x)$ decreasing?	$f(x)$ is decreasing when the gradient is negative
7.7	Using implicit differentiation, find $\dfrac{dy}{dx}$ for $x^2y + 3y = 3x2 + 5$	$\dfrac{dy}{dx} = \dfrac{2x(y+3)}{x^2 + 3}$
7.8	When is a curve convex?	A curve is convex if the second derivative is greater than zero, i.e. when the gradient is increasing
7.9	State the quotient rule for differentiating $y = \dfrac{u(x)}{v(x)}$	$\dfrac{dy}{dx} = \dfrac{v\dfrac{du}{dx} - u\dfrac{dv}{dx}}{v^2}$
7.10	How would you show that $\dfrac{d}{dx}\arcsin(x) = \dfrac{1}{\sqrt{1 - x^2}}$?	Use implicit differentiation on $\sin(y) = x$
7.11	How do you tell if $x = a$ is a local minimum of the function $f(x)$?	For $x = a$ to be a local minimum of $f(x)$, $f'(a) = 0$ and $f''(a) > 0$
7.12	Which differentiation rule would you use to differentiate $y = \sin^2(3x + 1)$?	The chain rule (twice)

Quiz 7: Differentiation

TRACKER

Quiz	Date	Score
1		
2		
3		
4		
5		
6		

Got it? ☐

Quiz 7: Differentiation

7.1	What is the formal definition of the derivative of $f(x)$?	
7.2	What is the derivative of $y = a^x$?	
7.3	What is the condition for a point x_1 to be a point of inflection for the function $f(x)$?	
7.4	For a curve C defined parametrically (i.e. with $x = f(t)$, $y = g(t)$) how would you find $\frac{dy}{dx}$?	
7.5	State the product rule for the function $y(x) = u(x)v(x)$	
7.6	When is a function $f(x)$ decreasing?	
7.7	Using implicit differentiation, find $\frac{dy}{dx}$ for $x^2y + 3y = 3x2 + 5$	
7.8	When is a curve convex?	
7.9	State the quotient rule for differentiating $y = \frac{u(x)}{v(x)}$	
7.10	How would you show that $\frac{d}{dx}\arcsin(x) = \frac{1}{\sqrt{1-x^2}}$?	
7.11	How do you tell if $x = a$ is a local minimum of the function $f(x)$?	
7.12	Which differentiation rule would you use to differentiate $y = \sin^2(3x + 1)$?	

Quiz 7: Differentiation

What is the condition for a point x_1 to be a point of inflection for the function $f(x)$?	
When is a function $f(x)$ decreasing?	
State the quotient rule for differentiating $y = \dfrac{u(x)}{v(x)}$	
Which differentiation rule would you use to differentiate $y = \sin^2(3x + 1)$?	
What is the derivative of $y = a^x$?	
For a curve C defined parametrically (i.e. with $x = f(t)$, $y = g(t)$) how would you find $\dfrac{dy}{dx}$?	
When is a curve convex?	
How would you show that $\dfrac{d}{dx} \arcsin(x) = \dfrac{1}{\sqrt{1-x^2}}$?	
What is the formal definition of the derivative of $f(x)$?	
State the product rule for the function $y(x) = u(x)v(x)$	
Using implicit differentiation, find $\dfrac{dy}{dx}$ for $x^2y + 3y = 3x2 + 5$	
How do you tell if $x = a$ is a local minimum of the function $f(x)$?	

Quiz 7: Differentiation

How would you show that $\frac{d}{dx}\arcsin(x) = \frac{1}{\sqrt{1-x^2}}$?	
What is the formal definition of the derivative of $f(x)$?	
State the product rule for the function $y(x) = u(x)v(x)$	
When is a function $f(x)$ decreasing?	
What is the derivative of $y = a^x$?	
State the quotient rule for differentiating $y = \frac{u(x)}{v(x)}$	
Using implicit differentiation, find $\frac{dy}{dx}$ for $x^2y + 3y = 3x2 + 5$	
How do you tell if $x = a$ is a local minimum of the function $f(x)$?	
When is a curve convex?	
Which differentiation rule would you use to differentiate $y = \sin^2(3x + 1)$?	
What is the condition for a point x_1 to be a point of inflection for the function $f(x)$?	
For a curve C defined parametrically (i.e. with $x = f(t)$, $y = g(t)$) how would you find $\frac{dy}{dx}$?	

Quiz 7: Differentiation

When is a function $f(x)$ decreasing?	
Which differentiation rule would you use to differentiate $y = \sin^2(3x + 1)$?	
What is the formal definition of the derivative of $f(x)$?	
What is the condition for a point x_1 to be a point of inflection for the function $f(x)$?	
Using implicit differentiation, find $\frac{dy}{dx}$ for $x^2y + 3y = 3x2 + 5$	
State the product rule for the function $y(x) = u(x)v(x)$	
How do you tell if $x = a$ is a local minimum of the function $f(x)$?	
When is a curve convex?	
For a curve C defined parametrically (i.e. with $x = f(t)$, $y = g(t)$) how would you find $\frac{dy}{dx}$?	
How would you show that $\frac{d}{dx} \arcsin(x) = \frac{1}{\sqrt{1 - x^2}}$?	
What is the derivative of $y = a^x$?	
State the quotient rule for differentiating $y = \frac{u(x)}{v(x)}$	

Quiz 7: Differentiation

What is the condition for a point x_1 to be a point of inflection for the function $f(x)$?	
When is a function $f(x)$ decreasing?	
State the quotient rule for differentiating $y = \dfrac{u(x)}{v(x)}$	
Which differentiation rule would you use to differentiate $y = \sin^2(3x + 1)$?	
What is the derivative of $y = a^x$?	
For a curve C defined parametrically (i.e. with $x = f(t)$, $y = g(t)$) how would you find $\dfrac{dy}{dx}$?	
When is a curve convex?	
How would you show that $\dfrac{d}{dx}\arcsin(x) = \dfrac{1}{\sqrt{1-x^2}}$?	
What is the formal definition of the derivative of $f(x)$?	
State the product rule for the function $y(x) = u(x)v(x)$	
Using implicit differentiation, find $\dfrac{dy}{dx}$ for $x^2y + 3y = 3x2 + 5$	
How do you tell if $x = a$ is a local minimum of the function $f(x)$?	

Quiz 7: Differentiation

How would you show that $\frac{d}{dx} \arcsin(x) = \frac{1}{\sqrt{1-x^2}}$?	
What is the formal definition of the derivative of $f(x)$?	
State the product rule for the function $y(x) = u(x)v(x)$	
When is a function $f(x)$ decreasing?	
What is the derivative of $y = a^x$?	
State the quotient rule for differentiating $y = \frac{u(x)}{v(x)}$	
Using implicit differentiation, find $\frac{dy}{dx}$ for $x^2y + 3y = 3x2 + 5$	
How do you tell if $x = a$ is a local minimum of the function $f(x)$?	
When is a curve convex?	
Which differentiation rule would you use to differentiate $y = \sin^2(3x+1)$?	
What is the condition for a point x_1 to be a point of inflection for the function $f(x)$?	
For a curve C defined parametrically (i.e. with $x = f(t)$, $y = g(t)$) how would you find $\frac{dy}{dx}$?	

Quiz 8: Integration

ANSWER KEY

8.1	What is the integral of x^n?	$\int x^n \, dx = \dfrac{1}{n+1} x^{n+1} + C$
8.2	What substitution could be used to find $\int x(x^2 - 4)^3 \, dx$?	$u = x^2 - 4$
8.3	What is the integral of $\dfrac{1}{x}$?	$\int \dfrac{1}{x} \, dx = \ln|x| + C$
8.4	How would you use integration by parts to integrate $\int x^2 e^x \, dx$?	Use integration by parts twice. First with $u = x^2$ to obtain a term, plus an integral where IBP with $u = x$
8.5	What does the definite integral $\int_a^b f(x) \, dx$ find?	It finds the area under the curve $f(x)$ between the limits $x = a$ and $x = b$. Care should be taken if the curve crosses the x-axis in the interval $[a,b]$
8.6	How would you solve the differential equation $\dfrac{dy}{dx} = f(x)g(y)$?	Separate the variables and integrate: $\int \dfrac{1}{g(y)} \, dy = \int f(x) \, dx$
8.7	How could you integrate $2\sin(5\theta)\sin(\theta)$?	Use the factor formulae to rewrite as $2\sin(5\theta)\sin(\theta) = \cos(6\theta) - \cos(4\theta)$ and then integrate
8.8	How could you integrate an expression of the form $\int k f'(x)(f(x))^n \, dx$?	Try $(f(x))^{n+1}$ and differentiate to check, then adjust any constant
8.9	How would you integrate $\ln(x)$?	Use integration by parts with $u = \ln(x)$ and $v(x) = 1$
8.10	What method would you use to find the integral of $f(x) = \dfrac{2x + 3}{(x + 3)(x + 4)}$?	Write $f(x) = \dfrac{5}{x+4} - \dfrac{3}{x+3}$ and then integrate term-by-term using the reverse chain rule and $\int \dfrac{1}{x} \, dx = \ln|x| + C$
8.11	What is $\int \sec(x)\tan(x) \, dx$?	$\int \sec(x)\tan(x) \, dx = \sec(x) + C$
8.12	If a curve is defined parametrically (i.e. both x and y are given in terms of a parameter t) what formula do you use to find the area under the curve?	$\int y \, dx = \int y \dfrac{dx}{dt} \, dt$

Quiz 8: Integration

TRACKER

Quiz	Date	Score
1		
2		
3		
4		
5		
6		

Got it? ☐

Quiz 8: Integration

8.1	What is the integral of x^n?	
8.2	What substitution could be used to find $\int x(x^2 - 4)^3 \, dx$?	
8.3	What is the integral of $\dfrac{1}{x}$?	
8.4	How would you use integration by parts to integrate $\int x^2 e^x \, dx$?	
8.5	What does the definite integral $\int_a^b f(x) \, dx$ find?	
8.6	How would you solve the differential equation $\dfrac{dy}{dx} = f(x)g(y)$?	
8.7	How could you integrate $2\sin(5\theta)\sin(\theta)$?	
8.8	How could you integrate an expression of the form $\int k f'(x)(f(x))^n \, dx$?	
8.9	How would you integrate $\ln(x)$?	
8.10	What method would you use to find the integral of $f(x) = \dfrac{2x + 3}{(x + 3)(x + 4)}$?	
8.11	What is $\int \sec(x)\tan(x) \, dx$?	
8.12	If a curve is defined parametrically (i.e. both x and y are given in terms of a parameter t) what formula do you use to find the area under the curve?	

Quiz 8: Integration

What is the integral of $\frac{1}{x}$?	
How would you solve the differential equation $\frac{dy}{dx} = f(x)g(y)$?	
How would you integrate $\ln(x)$?	
If a curve is defined parametrically (i.e. both x and y are given in terms of a parameter t) what formula do you use to find the area under the curve?	
What substitution could be used to find $\int x(x^2 - 4)^3 \, dx$?	
How would you use integration by parts to integrate $\int x^2 e^x \, dx$?	
How could you integrate an expression of the form $\int kf'(x)(f(x))^n \, dx$?	
What method would you use to find the integral of $f(x) = \frac{2x + 3}{(x + 3)(x + 4)}$?	
What is the integral of x^n?	
What does the definite integral $\int_a^b f(x) \, dx$ find?	
How could you integrate $2\sin(5\theta)\sin(\theta)$?	
What is $\int \sec(x)\tan(x) \, dx$?	

Quiz 8: Integration

What method would you use to find the integral of $f(x) = \dfrac{2x + 3}{(x + 3)(x + 4)}$?	
What is the integral of x^n?	
What does the definite integral $\int_a^b f(x)\,dx$ find?	
How would you solve the differential equation $\dfrac{dy}{dx} = f(x)g(y)$?	
What substitution could be used to find $\int x(x^2 - 4)^3\,dx$?	
How would you integrate $\ln(x)$?	
How could you integrate $2\sin(5\theta)\sin(\theta)$?	
What is $\int \sec(x)\tan(x)\,dx$?	
How could you integrate an expression of the form $\int kf'(x)(f(x))^n\,dx$?	
If a curve is defined parametrically (i.e. both x and y are given in terms of a parameter t) what formula do you use to find the area under the curve?	
What is the integral of $\dfrac{1}{x}$?	
How would you use integration by parts to integrate $\int x^2 e^x\,dx$?	

Quiz 8: Integration

How would you solve the differential equation $\frac{dy}{dx} = f(x)g(y)$?	
If a curve is defined parametrically (i.e. both x and y are given in terms of a parameter t) what formula do you use to find the area under the curve?	
What is the integral of x^n?	
What is the integral of $\frac{1}{x}$?	
How could you integrate $2\sin(5\theta)\sin(\theta)$?	
What does the definite integral $\int_a^b f(x)\,dx$ find?	
What is $\int \sec(x)\tan(x)\,dx$?	
How could you integrate an expression of the form $\int kf'(x)(f(x))^n\,dx$?	
How would you use integration by parts to integrate $\int x^2 e^x\,dx$?	
What method would you use to find the integral of $f(x) = \frac{2x+3}{(x+3)(x+4)}$?	
What substitution could be used to find $\int x(x^2-4)^3\,dx$?	
How would you integrate $\ln(x)$?	

Quiz 8: Integration

What is the integral of $\frac{1}{x}$?	
How would you solve the differential equation $\frac{dy}{dx} = f(x)g(y)$?	
How would you integrate $\ln(x)$?	
If a curve is defined parametrically (i.e. both x and y are given in terms of a parameter t) what formula do you use to find the area under the curve?	
What substitution could be used to find $\int x(x^2 - 4)^3 \, dx$?	
How would you use integration by parts to integrate $\int x^2 e^x \, dx$?	
How could you integrate an expression of the form $\int kf'(x)(f(x))^n \, dx$?	
What method would you use to find the integral of $f(x) = \frac{2x+3}{(x+3)(x+4)}$?	
What is the integral of x^n?	
What does the definite integral $\int_a^b f(x) \, dx$ find?	
How could you integrate $2\sin(5\theta)\sin(\theta)$?	
What is $\int \sec(x)\tan(x) \, dx$?	

Quiz 8: Integration

What method would you use to find the integral of $f(x) = \dfrac{2x+3}{(x+3)(x+4)}$?	
What is the integral of x^n?	
What does the definite integral $\int_a^b f(x)\,dx$ find?	
How would you solve the differential equation $\dfrac{dy}{dx} = f(x)g(y)$?	
What substitution could be used to find $\int x(x^2-4)^3\,dx$?	
How would you integrate $\ln(x)$?	
How could you integrate $2\sin(5\theta)\sin(\theta)$?	
What is $\int \sec(x)\tan(x)\,dx$?	
How could you integrate an expression of the form $\int kf'(x)(f(x))^n\,dx$?	
If a curve is defined parametrically (i.e. both x and y are given in terms of a parameter t) what formula do you use to find the area under the curve?	
What is the integral of $\dfrac{1}{x}$?	
How would you use integration by parts to integrate $\int x^2 e^x\,dx$?	

Quiz 9: Numerical methods

ANSWER KEY

9.1	How could you check for a root of $f(x)$ between $x = a$ and $x = b$, where $f(x)$ is continuous in this interval?	If the signs of $f(a)$ and $f(b)$ are different, the graph of $f(x)$ must have crossed the x-axis, hence there must be a root in the interval $[a, b]$
9.2	What is a cobweb diagram?	A visual demonstration of the convergence or divergence of a sequence of iterations $x_{n+1} = f(x_n)$
9.3	State the Newton-Raphson formula	$x_{n+1} = x_n - \dfrac{f(x_n)}{f'(x_n)}$
9.4	A fixed-point iteration $x_{n+1} = f(x_n)$ is used to try to find a root a. What conditions must be satisfied to ensure convergence?	The starting value should be sufficiently close to a. $\lvert f'(x) \rvert < 1$ in the search interval
9.5	If the Trapezium Rule is used to estimate the area under a concave down curve, will the value calculated be an underestimate or overestimate?	Underestimate
9.6	How do you calculate the percentage error made in an approximation?	% error $= \dfrac{\text{actual answer} - \text{estimate}}{\text{actual answer}} \times 100$
9.7	If the tangent to $f(x)$ is horizontal for an iterate x_n, why will the Newton-Raphson method fail to locate a root of $f(x)$?	If the tangent is horizontal it will not intersect the x-axis and so the next iterate x_{n+1} cannot be determined
9.8	How would you show that the result of a sequence of iterations, $x = 3.143$, is a root correct to 3 decimal places?	Check for a sign change between $x = 3.1425$ and $x = 3.1435$
9.9	State the formula for the Trapezium Rule	$\int_a^b y\,dx = \dfrac{(b-a)}{2n}[y_0 + y_n + 2(y_1 + y_2 + \ldots + y_{n-1})]$
9.10	What would improve the accuracy of an approximation made by the Trapezium Rule?	Increasing the number of "strips" used (i.e. reducing the strip width h)
9.11	When using the sign change method to demonstrate that there is a root of $f(x)$ between $x = a$ and $x = b$, what problem could occur if the interval is too big?	Both $f(a)$ and $f(b)$ may be the same, not because there is no root, but because there are an even number of roots in the interval
9.12	If the Trapezium Rule is used to estimate the area under a concave up curve, will the value calculated be an underestimate or overestimate?	Overestimate

Quiz 9: Numerical methods

TRACKER

Quiz	Date	Score
1		
2		
3		
4		
5		
6		

Got it? ☐

Quiz 9: Numerical methods

9.1	How could you check for a root of $f(x)$ between $x = a$ and $x = b$, where $f(x)$ is continuous in this interval?	
9.2	What is a cobweb diagram?	
9.3	State the Newton-Raphson formula	
9.4	A fixed-point iteration $x_{n+1} = f(x_n)$ is used to try to find a root a. What conditions must be satisfied to ensure convergence?	
9.5	If the Trapezium Rule is used to estimate the area under a concave down curve, will the value calculated be an underestimate or overestimate?	
9.6	How do you calculate the percentage error made in an approximation?	
9.7	If the tangent to $f(x)$ is horizontal for an iterate x_n, why will the Newton-Raphson method fail to locate a root of $f(x)$?	
9.8	How would you show that the result of a sequence of iterations, $x = 3.143$, is a root correct to 3 decimal places?	
9.9	State the formula for the Trapezium Rule	
9.10	What would improve the accuracy of an approximation made by the Trapezium Rule?	
9.11	When using the sign change method to demonstrate that there is a root of $f(x)$ between $x = a$ and $x = b$, what problem could occur if the interval is too big?	
9.12	If the Trapezium Rule is used to estimate the area under a concave up curve, will the value calculated be an underestimate or overestimate?	

Quiz 9: Numerical methods

State the Newton-Raphson formula	
How do you calculate the percentage error made in an approximation?	
State the formula for the Trapezium Rule	
If the Trapezium Rule is used to estimate the area under a concave up curve, will the value calculated be an underestimate or overestimate?	
What is a cobweb diagram?	
A fixed-point iteration $x_{n+1} = f(x_n)$ is used to try to find a root a. What conditions must be satisfied to ensure convergence?	
How would you show that the result of a sequence of iterations, $x = 3.143$, is a root correct to 3 decimal places?	
What would improve the accuracy of an approximation made by the Trapezium Rule?	
How could you check for a root of $f(x)$ between $x = a$ and $x = b$, where $f(x)$ is continuous in this interval?	
If the Trapezium Rule is used to estimate the area under a concave down curve, will the value calculated be an underestimate or overestimate?	
If the tangent to $f(x)$ is horizontal for an iterate x_n, why will the Newton-Raphson method fail to locate a root of $f(x)$?	
When using the sign change method to demonstrate that there is a root of $f(x)$ between $x = a$ and $x = b$, what problem could occur if the interval is too big?	

Quiz 9: Numerical methods

What would improve the accuracy of an approximation made by the Trapezium Rule?	
How could you check for a root of $f(x)$ between $x = a$ and $x = b$, where $f(x)$ is continuous in this interval?	
If the Trapezium Rule is used to estimate the area under a concave down curve, will the value calculated be an underestimate or overestimate?	
How do you calculate the percentage error made in an approximation?	
What is a cobweb diagram?	
State the formula for the Trapezium Rule	
If the tangent to $f(x)$ is horizontal for an iterate x_n, why will the Newton-Raphson method fail to locate a root of $f(x)$?	
When using the sign change method to demonstrate that there is a root of $f(x)$ between $x = a$ and $x = b$, what problem could occur if the interval is too big?	
How would you show that the result of a sequence of iterations, $x = 3.143$, is a root correct to 3 decimal places?	
If the Trapezium Rule is used to estimate the area under a concave up curve, will the value calculated be an underestimate or overestimate?	
State the Newton-Raphson formula	
A fixed-point iteration $x_{n+1} = f(x_n)$ is used to try to find a root a. What conditions must be satisfied to ensure convergence?	

Quiz 9: Numerical methods

How do you calculate the percentage error made in an approximation?	
If the Trapezium Rule is used to estimate the area under a concave up curve, will the value calculated be an underestimate or overestimate?	
How could you check for a root of $f(x)$ between $x = a$ and $x = b$, where $f(x)$ is continuous in this interval?	
State the Newton-Raphson formula	
If the tangent to $f(x)$ is horizontal for an iterate x_n, why will the Newton-Raphson method fail to locate a root of $f(x)$?	
If the Trapezium Rule is used to estimate the area under a concave down curve, will the value calculated be an underestimate or overestimate?	
When using the sign change method to demonstrate that there is a root of $f(x)$ between $x = a$ and $x = b$, what problem could occur if the interval is too big?	
How would you show that the result of a sequence of iterations, $x = 3.143$, is a root correct to 3 decimal places?	
A fixed-point iteration $x_{n+1} = f(x_n)$ is used to try to find a root a. What conditions must be satisfied to ensure convergence?	
What would improve the accuracy of an approximation made by the Trapezium Rule?	
What is a cobweb diagram?	
State the formula for the Trapezium Rule	

Quiz 9: Numerical methods

State the Newton-Raphson formula	
How do you calculate the percentage error made in an approximation?	
State the formula for the Trapezium Rule	
If the Trapezium Rule is used to estimate the area under a concave up curve, will the value calculated be an underestimate or overestimate?	
What is a cobweb diagram?	
A fixed-point iteration $x_{n+1} = f(x_n)$ is used to try to find a root a. What conditions must be satisfied to ensure convergence?	
How would you show that the result of a sequence of iterations, $x = 3.143$, is a root correct to 3 decimal places?	
What would improve the accuracy of an approximation made by the Trapezium Rule?	
How could you check for a root of $f(x)$ between $x = a$ and $x = b$, where $f(x)$ is continuous in this interval?	
If the Trapezium Rule is used to estimate the area under a concave down curve, will the value calculated be an underestimate or overestimate?	
If the tangent to $f(x)$ is horizontal for an iterate x_n, why will the Newton-Raphson method fail to locate a root of $f(x)$?	
When using the sign change method to demonstrate that there is a root of $f(x)$ between $x = a$ and $x = b$, what problem could occur if the interval is too big?	

Quiz 9: Numerical methods

What would improve the accuracy of an approximation made by the Trapezium Rule?	
How could you check for a root of $f(x)$ between $x = a$ and $x = b$, where $f(x)$ is continuous in this interval?	
If the Trapezium Rule is used to estimate the area under a concave down curve, will the value calculated be an underestimate or overestimate?	
How do you calculate the percentage error made in an approximation?	
What is a cobweb diagram?	
State the formula for the Trapezium Rule	
If the tangent to $f(x)$ is horizontal for an iterate x_n, why will the Newton-Raphson method fail to locate a root of $f(x)$?	
When using the sign change method to demonstrate that there is a root of $f(x)$ between $x = a$ and $x = b$, what problem could occur if the interval is too big?	
How would you show that the result of a sequence of iterations, $x = 3.143$, is a root correct to 3 decimal places?	
If the Trapezium Rule is used to estimate the area under a concave up curve, will the value calculated be an underestimate or overestimate?	
State the Newton-Raphson formula	
A fixed-point iteration $x_{n+1} = f(x_n)$ is used to try to find a root a. What conditions must be satisfied to ensure convergence?	

Quiz 10: Vectors

ANSWER KEY

10.1	For the vector **a**, how do you calculate $\|\mathbf{a}\|$?	Use Pythagoras' Theorem
10.2	What is the magnitude of the vector $3\mathbf{i} + 4\mathbf{j}$?	5
10.3	How do you check if two vectors are parallel?	Vectors are parallel if they are scalar multiples of each other
10.4	How do you find the distance between a point with position vector $a_1\mathbf{i} + a_2\mathbf{j} + a_3\mathbf{k}$ and a point with position vector $b_1\mathbf{i} + b_2\mathbf{j} + b_3\mathbf{k}$?	$\sqrt{(a_1 - b_1)^2 + (a_2 - b_2)^2 + (a_3 - b_3)^2}$
10.5	What is a unit vector?	A vector with magnitude 1
10.6	What is a vector?	A quantity with both size and direction
10.7	What trigonometric rule can be used to find the angle between two vectors?	The cosine rule
10.8	What are the unit vectors in three dimensions?	**i**, **j** and **k**
10.9	Write in column form the vector $\mathbf{a} = 3\mathbf{i} + 2\mathbf{j} - 4\mathbf{k}$	$\mathbf{a} = \begin{pmatrix} 3 \\ 2 \\ -4 \end{pmatrix}$
10.10	How do you find the unit vector in the direction of **a**?	$\hat{\mathbf{a}} = \dfrac{\mathbf{a}}{\|\mathbf{a}\|}$
10.11	What does it mean when you are asked to "resolve" a vector where you are given the magnitude and direction?	It means to write the vector in terms of the components in the direction **i** and **j**
10.12	What is a position vector?	A position vector describes the position of a point with reference to a fixed origin O

Quiz 10: Vectors

TRACKER

Quiz	Date	Score
1		
2		
3		
4		
5		
6		

Got it? ☐

Quiz 10: Vectors

10.1	For the vector **a**, how do you calculate $|\mathbf{a}|$?	
10.2	What is the magnitude of the vector $3\mathbf{i} + 4\mathbf{j}$?	
10.3	How do you check if two vectors are parallel?	
10.4	How do you find the distance between a point with position vector $a_1\mathbf{i} + a_2\mathbf{j} + a_3\mathbf{k}$ and a point with position vector $b_1\mathbf{i} + b_2\mathbf{j} + b_3\mathbf{k}$?	
10.5	What is a unit vector?	
10.6	What is a vector?	
10.7	What trigonometric rule can be used to find the angle between two vectors?	
10.8	What are the unit vectors in three dimensions?	
10.9	Write in column form the vector $\mathbf{a} = 3\mathbf{i} + 2\mathbf{j} - 4\mathbf{k}$	
10.10	How do you find the unit vector in the direction of **a**?	
10.11	What does it mean when you are asked to "resolve" a vector where you are given the magnitude and direction?	
10.12	What is a position vector?	

Quiz 10: Vectors

How do you check if two vectors are parallel?	
What is a vector?	
Write in column form the vector $\mathbf{a} = 3\mathbf{i} + 2\mathbf{j} - 4\mathbf{k}$	
What is a position vector?	
What is the magnitude of the vector $3\mathbf{i} + 4\mathbf{j}$?	
How do you find the distance between a point with position vector $a_1\mathbf{i} + a_2\mathbf{j} + a_3\mathbf{k}$ and a point with position vector $b_1\mathbf{i} + b_2\mathbf{j} + b_3\mathbf{k}$?	
What are the unit vectors in three dimensions?	
How do you find the unit vector in the direction of $\mathbf{a}$?	
For the vector $\mathbf{a}$, how do you calculate $|\mathbf{a}|$?	
What is a unit vector?	
What trigonometric rule can be used to find the angle between two vectors?	
What does it mean when you are asked to "resolve" a vector where you are given the magnitude and direction?	

Quiz 10: Vectors

How do you find the unit vector in the direction of **a**?	
For the vector **a**, how do you calculate |**a**|?	
What is a unit vector?	
What is a vector?	
What is the magnitude of the vector $3\mathbf{i} + 4\mathbf{j}$?	
Write in column form the vector $\mathbf{a} = 3\mathbf{i} + 2\mathbf{j} - 4\mathbf{k}$	
What trigonometric rule can be used to find the angle between two vectors?	
What does it mean when you are asked to "resolve" a vector where you are given the magnitude and direction?	
What are the unit vectors in three dimensions?	
What is a position vector?	
How do you check if two vectors are parallel?	
How do you find the distance between a point with position vector $a_1\mathbf{i} + a_2\mathbf{j} + a_3\mathbf{k}$ and a point with position vector $b_1\mathbf{i} + b_2\mathbf{j} + b_3\mathbf{k}$?	

Quiz 10: Vectors

What is a vector?	
What is a position vector?	
For the vector **a**, how do you calculate $|\mathbf{a}|$?	
How do you check if two vectors are parallel?	
What trigonometric rule can be used to find the angle between two vectors?	
What is a unit vector?	
What does it mean when you are asked to "resolve" a vector where you are given the magnitude and direction?	
What are the unit vectors in three dimensions?	
How do you find the distance between a point with position vector $a_1\mathbf{i} + a_2\mathbf{j} + a_3\mathbf{k}$ and a point with position vector $b_1\mathbf{i} + b_2\mathbf{j} + b_3\mathbf{k}$?	
How do you find the unit vector in the direction of **a**?	
What is the magnitude of the vector $3\mathbf{i} + 4\mathbf{j}$?	
Write in column form the vector $\mathbf{a} = 3\mathbf{i} + 2\mathbf{j} - 4\mathbf{k}$	

Quiz 10: Vectors

How do you check if two vectors are parallel?	
What is a vector?	
Write in column form the vector $\mathbf{a} = 3\mathbf{i} + 2\mathbf{j} - 4\mathbf{k}$	
What is a position vector?	
What is the magnitude of the vector $3\mathbf{i} + 4\mathbf{j}$?	
How do you find the distance between a point with position vector $a_1\mathbf{i} + a_2\mathbf{j} + a_3\mathbf{k}$ and a point with position vector $b_1\mathbf{i} + b_2\mathbf{j} + b_3\mathbf{k}$?	
What are the unit vectors in three dimensions?	
How do you find the unit vector in the direction of $\mathbf{a}$?	
For the vector $\mathbf{a}$, how do you calculate $|\mathbf{a}|$?	
What is a unit vector?	
What trigonometric rule can be used to find the angle between two vectors?	
What does it mean when you are asked to "resolve" a vector where you are given the magnitude and direction?	

Quiz 10: Vectors

How do you find the unit vector in the direction of **a**?	
For the vector **a**, how do you calculate $|\mathbf{a}|$?	
What is a unit vector?	
What is a vector?	
What is the magnitude of the vector $3\mathbf{i} + 4\mathbf{j}$?	
Write in column form the vector $\mathbf{a} = 3\mathbf{i} + 2\mathbf{j} - 4\mathbf{k}$	
What trigonometric rule can be used to find the angle between two vectors?	
What does it mean when you are asked to "resolve" a vector where you are given the magnitude and direction?	
What are the unit vectors in three dimensions?	
What is a position vector?	
How do you check if two vectors are parallel?	
How do you find the distance between a point with position vector $a_1\mathbf{i} + a_2\mathbf{j} + a_3\mathbf{k}$ and a point with position vector $b_1\mathbf{i} + b_2\mathbf{j} + b_3\mathbf{k}$?	

Quiz 11: Statistical sampling

ANSWER KEY

11.1	What is a census?	A census is the procedure of systematically acquiring and recording information about the members of a given population
11.2	How do you calculate the size of a sample category when using stratified sampling?	Divide the size of the category in the population by the total size of the population and then multiply by the total sample size
11.3	Describe systematic sampling	Every nth member of a population is selected
11.4	What is a sampling frame?	A full list of sampling units
11.5	What does the phrase "random sampling" mean?	All members of a population are equally likely to be selected
11.6	Describe opportunity sampling	The sample is collected at a given place and time convenient for the sampler
11.7	What does it mean to say that a population is infinite?	When you cannot know how many members of a population there are
11.8	What is a biased sample?	A sample that isn't representative of the population
11.9	How do you select a quota sample?	You divide the population into categories, give each category a quota and then collect data until the quotas for all categories are filled
11.10	State two disadvantages of opportunity sampling	It isn't random and can lead to biased samples
11.11	What is a sampling unit?	The individual members of the population that are to be sampled
11.12	What is an advantage of cluster sampling?	Often quicker or cheaper than other methods

Quiz 11: Statistical sampling

TRACKER

Quiz	Date	Score
1		
2		
3		
4		
5		
6		

Got it? ☐

Quiz 11: Statistical sampling

11.1	What is a census?	
11.2	How do you calculate the size of a sample category when using stratified sampling?	
11.3	Describe systematic sampling	
11.4	What is a sampling frame?	
11.5	What does the phrase "random sampling" mean?	
11.6	Describe opportunity sampling	
11.7	What does it mean to say that a population is infinite?	
11.8	What is a biased sample?	
11.9	How do you select a quota sample?	
11.10	State two disadvantages of opportunity sampling	
11.11	What is a sampling unit?	
11.12	What is an advantage of cluster sampling?	

Quiz 11: Statistical sampling

Describe systematic sampling	
Describe opportunity sampling	
How do you select a quota sample?	
What is an advantage of cluster sampling?	
How do you calculate the size of a sample category when using stratified sampling?	
What is a sampling frame?	
What is a biased sample?	
State two disadvantages of opportunity sampling	
What is a census?	
What does the phrase "random sampling" mean?	
What does it mean to say that a population is infinite?	
What is a sampling unit?	

Quiz 11: Statistical sampling

State two disadvantages of opportunity sampling	
What is a census?	
What does the phrase "random sampling" mean?	
Describe opportunity sampling	
How do you calculate the size of a sample category when using stratified sampling?	
How do you select a quota sample?	
What does it mean to say that a population is infinite?	
What is a sampling unit?	
What is a biased sample?	
What is an advantage of cluster sampling?	
Describe systematic sampling	
What is a sampling frame?	

Quiz 11: Statistical sampling

Describe opportunity sampling	
What is an advantage of cluster sampling?	
What is a census?	
Describe systematic sampling	
What does it mean to say that a population is infinite?	
What does the phrase "random sampling" mean?	
What is a sampling unit?	
What is a biased sample?	
What is a sampling frame?	
State two disadvantages of opportunity sampling	
How do you calculate the size of a sample category when using stratified sampling?	
How do you select a quota sample?	

Quiz 11: Statistical sampling

Describe systematic sampling	
Describe opportunity sampling	
How do you select a quota sample?	
What is an advantage of cluster sampling?	
How do you calculate the size of a sample category when using stratified sampling?	
What is a sampling frame?	
What is a biased sample?	
State two disadvantages of opportunity sampling	
What is a census?	
What does the phrase "random sampling" mean?	
What does it mean to say that a population is infinite?	
What is a sampling unit?	

Quiz 11: Statistical sampling

State two disadvantages of opportunity sampling	
What is a census?	
What does the phrase "random sampling" mean?	
Describe opportunity sampling	
How do you calculate the size of a sample category when using stratified sampling?	
How do you select a quota sample?	
What does it mean to say that a population is infinite?	
What is a sampling unit?	
What is a biased sample?	
What is an advantage of cluster sampling?	
Describe systematic sampling	
What is a sampling frame?	

Quiz 12: Data presentation and interpretation

ANSWER KEY

12.1	What is the standard deviation of a set of data?	A measure of how spread out the data is from the mean
12.2	Define extrapolation	Extrapolation is when you use data to make inferences outside of the range of the known data. These predictions can be unreliable
12.3	For data that is presented in groups, can you find the exact value of the mean?	No, you can only estimate the mean by making use of the midpoints of the groups
12.4	For a histogram, how do you calculate the frequency density?	frequency density = $\dfrac{\text{frequency}}{\text{class width}}$
12.5	How do you construct a cumulative frequency plot?	From a frequency table you can construct the cumulative frequency column. Then plot points at $(x, \text{cumulative frequency at } x)$ before joining with a smooth curve
12.6	What is the difference between μ and $\bar{x}$?	The population mean is denoted by μ, whereas $\bar{x}$ is a sample mean
12.7	What is correlation?	A measure of how linked two variables are
12.8	For data given in a frequency table, what formula could you use to calculate the variance?	$\dfrac{\Sigma fx^2}{\Sigma f} - \bar{x}^2$ where $\bar{x} = \dfrac{\Sigma fx}{\Sigma f}$
12.9	How could you compare two distributions?	Box plots are ideal for comparing data from two distributions as you can easily comment on the location and spread of the data
12.10	Shoe size is found to be highly correlated with mathematics scores in a Year 8 test. What can be said about the influence of shoe size on a student's mathematics ability?	Nothing. Correlation does not necessarily imply causation
12.11	What is the mode of a set of data?	The most frequently occurring piece of data
12.12	What is signified by a PMCC of negative 1?	This is perfect negative correlation. All points lie exactly on a straight line with negative gradient

Quiz 12: Data presentation and interpretation

TRACKER

Quiz	Date	Score
1		
2		
3		
4		
5		
6		

Got it? ☐

Quiz 12: Data presentation and interpretation

12.1	What is the standard deviation of a set of data?	
12.2	Define extrapolation	
12.3	For data that is presented in groups, can you find the exact value of the mean?	
12.4	For a histogram, how do you calculate the frequency density?	
12.5	How do you construct a cumulative frequency plot?	
12.6	What is the difference between μ and $\bar{x}$?	
12.7	What is correlation?	
12.8	For data given in a frequency table, what formula could you use to calculate the variance?	
12.9	How could you compare two distributions?	
12.10	Shoe size is found to be highly correlated with mathematics scores in a Year 8 test. What can be said about the influence of shoe size on a student's mathematics ability?	
12.11	What is the mode of a set of data?	
12.12	What is signified by a PMCC of negative 1?	

Quiz 12: Data presentation and interpretation

For data that is presented in groups, can you find the exact value of the mean?	
What is the difference between μ and $\bar{x}$?	
How could you compare two distributions?	
What is signified by a PMCC of negative 1?	
Define extrapolation	
For a histogram, how do you calculate the frequency density?	
For data given in a frequency table, what formula could you use to calculate the variance?	
Shoe size is found to be highly correlated with mathematics scores in a Year 8 test. What can be said about the influence of shoe size on a student's mathematics ability?	
What is the standard deviation of a set of data?	
How do you construct a cumulative frequency plot?	
What is correlation?	
What is the mode of a set of data?	

Quiz 12: Data presentation and interpretation

Shoe size is found to be highly correlated with mathematics scores in a Year 8 test. What can be said about the influence of shoe size on a student's mathematics ability?	
What is the standard deviation of a set of data?	
How do you construct a cumulative frequency plot?	
What is the difference between μ and $\bar{x}$?	
Define extrapolation	
How could you compare two distributions?	
What is correlation?	
What is the mode of a set of data?	
For data given in a frequency table, what formula could you use to calculate the variance?	
What is signified by a PMCC of negative 1?	
For data that is presented in groups, can you find the exact value of the mean?	
For a histogram, how do you calculate the frequency density?	

Quiz 12: Data presentation and interpretation

What is the difference between μ and $\bar{x}$?	
What is signified by a PMCC of negative 1?	
What is the standard deviation of a set of data?	
For data that is presented in groups, can you find the exact value of the mean?	
What is correlation?	
How do you construct a cumulative frequency plot?	
What is the mode of a set of data?	
For data given in a frequency table, what formula could you use to calculate the variance?	
For a histogram, how do you calculate the frequency density?	
Shoe size is found to be highly correlated with mathematics scores in a Year 8 test. What can be said about the influence of shoe size on a student's mathematics ability?	
Define extrapolation	
How could you compare two distributions?	

Quiz 12: Data presentation and interpretation

For data that is presented in groups, can you find the exact value of the mean?	
What is the difference between μ and $\bar{x}$?	
How could you compare two distributions?	
What is signified by a PMCC of negative 1?	
Define extrapolation	
For a histogram, how do you calculate the frequency density?	
For data given in a frequency table, what formula could you use to calculate the variance?	
Shoe size is found to be highly correlated with mathematics scores in a Year 8 test. What can be said about the influence of shoe size on a student's mathematics ability?	
What is the standard deviation of a set of data?	
How do you construct a cumulative frequency plot?	
What is correlation?	
What is the mode of a set of data?	

Quiz 12: Data presentation and interpretation

Shoe size is found to be highly correlated with mathematics scores in a Year 8 test. What can be said about the influence of shoe size on a student's mathematics ability?	
What is the standard deviation of a set of data?	
How do you construct a cumulative frequency plot?	
What is the difference between μ and $\bar{x}$?	
Define extrapolation	
How could you compare two distributions?	
What is correlation?	
What is the mode of a set of data?	
For data given in a frequency table, what formula could you use to calculate the variance?	
What is signified by a PMCC of negative 1?	
For data that is presented in groups, can you find the exact value of the mean?	
For a histogram, how do you calculate the frequency density?	

Quiz 13: Probability

ANSWER KEY

13.1	How do you denote the union of two sets?	$A \cup B$
13.2	How do you denote the complement of event A and what does it mean?	The complement of A is denoted A' and is anything in the sample space that is not in event A
13.3	What do you do with the probabilities as you move along the branches of a tree diagram?	You multiply the probabilities
13.4	How can you tell if two events A and B are independent?	If A and B are independent then $P(A \mid B) = P(A)$
13.5	Complete the following identity $P(A \cup B) = P(A) + P(B) -$	$P(A \cup B) = P(A) + P(B) - P(A \cap B)$
13.6	How do you calculate the probability of an event happening?	You divide the number of outcomes where the event occurs by the total number of possible outcomes
13.7	How is $P(B \mid A)$ related to $P(A)$?	$P(B \mid A) = \dfrac{P(A \cap B)}{P(A)}$
13.8	What does it mean for two events A and B to be mutually exclusive?	$P(A \cap B) = 0$
13.9	What does $A \cap B$ mean for two sets A and B?	The intersection of sets A and B. This is the set of members that are both in set A and in set B
13.10	What does $P(B \mid A)$ mean?	The probability of event B happening given that event A has already happened
13.11	For independent events A and B, $P(A \cap B) =$	$P(A \cap B) = P(A)P(B)$
13.12	If the probability of event A happening is P, how do you work out the probability of event A not happening?	$1 - p$

Quiz 13: Probability

TRACKER

Quiz	Date	Score
1		
2		
3		
4		
5		
6		

Got it? ☐

Quiz 13: Probability

13.1	How do you denote the union of two sets?	
13.2	How do you denote the complement of event A and what does it mean?	
13.3	What do you do with the probabilities as you move along the branches of a tree diagram?	
13.4	How can you tell if two events A and B are independent?	
13.5	Complete the following identity $P(A \cup B) = P(A) + P(B) -$	
13.6	How do you calculate the probability of an event happening?	
13.7	How is $P(B \mid A)$ related to $P(A)$?	
13.8	What does it mean for two events A and B to be mutually exclusive?	
13.9	What does $A \cap B$ mean for two sets A and B?	
13.10	What does $P(B \mid A)$ mean?	
13.11	For independent events A and B, $P(A \cap B) =$	
13.12	If the probability of event A happening is P, how do you work out the probability of event A not happening?	

Quiz 13: Probability

What do you do with the probabilities as you move along the branches of a tree diagram?	
How do you calculate the probability of an event happening?	
What does $A \cap B$ mean for two sets A and B?	
If the probability of event A happening is P, how do you work out the probability of event A not happening?	
How do you denote the complement of event A and what does it mean?	
How can you tell if two events A and B are independent?	
What does it mean for two events A and B to be mutually exclusive?	
What does $P(B \mid A)$ mean?	
How do you denote the union of two sets?	
Complete the following identity $P(A \cup B) = P(A) + P(B) -$	
How is $P(B \mid A)$ related to $P(A)$?	
For independent events A and B, $P(A \cap B) =$	

Quiz 13: Probability

What does $P(B \mid A)$ mean?	
How do you denote the union of two sets?	
Complete the following identity $P(A \cup B) = P(A) + P(B) -$	
How do you calculate the probability of an event happening?	
How do you denote the complement of event A and what does it mean?	
What does $A \cap B$ mean for two sets A and B?	
How is $P(B \mid A)$ related to $P(A)$?	
For independent events A and B, $P(A \cap B) =$	
What does it mean for two events A and B to be mutually exclusive?	
If the probability of event A happening is P, how do you work out the probability of event A not happening?	
What do you do with the probabilities as you move along the branches of a tree diagram?	
How can you tell if two events A and B are independent?	

Quiz 13: Probability

How do you calculate the probability of an event happening?	
If the probability of event A happening is P, how do you work out the probability of event A not happening?	
How do you denote the union of two sets?	
What do you do with the probabilities as you move along the branches of a tree diagram?	
How is $P(B \mid A)$ related to $P(A)$?	
Complete the following identity $P(A \cup B) = P(A) + P(B) -$	
For independent events A and B, $P(A \cap B) =$	
What does it mean for two events A and B to be mutually exclusive?	
How can you tell if two events A and B are independent?	
What does $P(B \mid A)$ mean?	
How do you denote the complement of event A and what does it mean?	
What does $A \cap B$ mean for two sets A and B?	

Quiz 13: Probability

What do you do with the probabilities as you move along the branches of a tree diagram?	
How do you calculate the probability of an event happening?	
What does $A \cap B$ mean for two sets A and B?	
If the probability of event A happening is P, how do you work out the probability of event A not happening?	
How do you denote the complement of event A and what does it mean?	
How can you tell if two events A and B are independent?	
What does it mean for two events A and B to be mutually exclusive?	
What does $P(B \mid A)$ mean?	
How do you denote the union of two sets?	
Complete the following identity $P(A \cup B) = P(A) + P(B) -$	
How is $P(B \mid A)$ related to $P(A)$?	
For independent events A and B, $P(A \cap B) =$	

Quiz 13: Probability

What does $P(B \mid A)$ mean?	
How do you denote the union of two sets?	
Complete the following identity $P(A \cup B) = P(A) + P(B) -$	
How do you calculate the probability of an event happening?	
How do you denote the complement of event A and what does it mean?	
What does $A \cap B$ mean for two sets A and B?	
How is $P(B \mid A)$ related to $P(A)$?	
For independent events A and B, $P(A \cap B) =$	
What does it mean for two events A and B to be mutually exclusive?	
If the probability of event A happening is P, how do you work out the probability of event A not happening?	
What do you do with the probabilities as you move along the branches of a tree diagram?	
How can you tell if two events A and B are independent?	

Quiz 14: Statistical distributions

ANSWER KEY

14.1	$\sum_{\text{all } x} P(X = x) = ?$	1
14.2	How do we denote a normal distribution with mean μ and standard deviation σ?	$X \sim N(\mu, \sigma^2)$
14.3	What does $P(X = x)$ mean?	The probability that the random variable X takes the specific value x
14.4	For the binomial distribution $X \sim B(n, p)$, what is the mean and what is the variance?	The mean is np and the variance is $np(1 - p)$ (sometimes this is written as npq where $q = 1 - p$)
14.5	For the normal distribution $X \sim N(\mu, \sigma^2)$, where are the points of inflection?	At $x = \mu \pm \sigma$
14.6	For a normal distribution, how much of the area under the curve lies within 1 standard deviation of the mean?	68%
14.7	How many ways can n different objects be arranged if r of them are the same?	$\dfrac{n!}{r!}$
14.8	How do you transform the normal distribution $X \sim N(\mu, \sigma^2)$ to the standard normal distribution Z?	$Z \sim \dfrac{X - \mu}{\sigma}$ where $Z \sim N(0, 1)$
14.9	For a discrete distribution, what is the cumulative distribution function?	It gives the probability that the random variable X will take a value less than, or equal, to a given value
14.10	When can you use the normal distribution to approximate the binomial distribution $X \sim B(n, p)$?	If n is large and $p \approx 0.5$
14.11	Which continuous probability distribution has a symmetrical bell-shaped curve?	The normal distribution
14.12	What is a discrete random variable?	A discrete random variable can only take particular values

Quiz 14: Statistical distributions

TRACKER

Quiz	Date	Score
1		
2		
3		
4		
5		
6		

Got it? ☐

Quiz 14: Statistical distributions

14.1	$\sum_{\text{all } x} P(X = x) = ?$	
14.2	How do we denote a normal distribution with mean μ and standard deviation σ?	
14.3	What does $P(X = x)$ mean?	
14.4	For the binomial distribution $X \sim B(n, p)$, what is the mean and what is the variance?	
14.5	For the normal distribution $X \sim N(\mu, \sigma^2)$, where are the points of inflection?	
14.6	For a normal distribution, how much of the area under the curve lies within 1 standard deviation of the mean?	
14.7	How many ways can n different objects be arranged if r of them are the same?	
14.8	How do you transform the normal distribution $X \sim N(\mu, \sigma^2)$ to the standard normal distribution Z?	
14.9	For a discrete distribution, what is the cumulative distribution function?	
14.10	When can you use the normal distribution to approximate the binomial distribution $X \sim B(n, p)$?	
14.11	Which continuous probability distribution has a symmetrical bell-shaped curve?	
14.12	What is a discrete random variable?	

Quiz 14: Statistical distributions

What does $P(X = x)$ mean?	
For a normal distribution, how much of the area under the curve lies within 1 standard deviation of the mean?	
For a discrete distribution, what is the cumulative distribution function?	
What is a discrete random variable?	
How do we denote a normal distribution with mean μ and standard deviation σ?	
For the binomial distribution $X \sim B(n, p)$, what is the mean and what is the variance?	
How do you transform the normal distribution $X \sim N(\mu, \sigma^2)$ to the standard normal distribution Z?	
When can you use the normal distribution to approximate the binomial distribution $X \sim B(n, p)$?	
$\sum_{\text{all } x} P(X = x) = ?$	
For the normal distribution $X \sim N(\mu, \sigma^2)$, where are the points of inflection?	
How many ways can n different objects be arranged if r of them are the same?	
Which continuous probability distribution has a symmetrical bell-shaped curve?	

Quiz 14: Statistical distributions

When can you use the normal distribution to approximate the binomial distribution $X \sim B(n, p)$?	
$\sum_{\text{all } x} P(X = x) = ?$	
For the normal distribution $X \sim N(\mu, \sigma^2)$, where are the points of inflection?	
For a normal distribution, how much of the area under the curve lies within 1 standard deviation of the mean?	
How do we denote a normal distribution with mean μ and standard deviation σ?	
For a discrete distribution, what is the cumulative distribution function?	
How many ways can n different objects be arranged if r of them are the same?	
Which continuous probability distribution has a symmetrical bell-shaped curve?	
How do you transform the normal distribution $X \sim N(\mu, \sigma^2)$ to the standard normal distribution Z?	
What is a discrete random variable?	
What does $P(X = x)$ mean?	
For the binomial distribution $X \sim B(n, p)$, what is the mean and what is the variance?	

Quiz 14: Statistical distributions

For a normal distribution, how much of the area under the curve lies within 1 standard deviation of the mean?	
What is a discrete random variable?	
$\sum_{\text{all } x} P(X = x) = ?$	
What does $P(X = x)$ mean?	
How many ways can n different objects be arranged if r of them are the same?	
For the normal distribution $X \sim N(\mu, \sigma^2)$, where are the points of inflection?	
Which continuous probability distribution has a symmetrical bell-shaped curve?	
How do you transform the normal distribution $X \sim N(\mu, \sigma^2)$ to the standard normal distribution Z?	
For the binomial distribution $X \sim B(n, p)$, what is the mean and what is the variance?	
When can you use the normal distribution to approximate the binomial distribution $X \sim B(n, p)$?	
How do we denote a normal distribution with mean μ and standard deviation σ?	
For a discrete distribution, what is the cumulative distribution function?	

Quiz 14: Statistical distributions

What does P(X = x) mean?	
For a normal distribution, how much of the area under the curve lies within 1 standard deviation of the mean?	
For a discrete distribution, what is the cumulative distribution function?	
What is a discrete random variable?	
How do we denote a normal distribution with mean μ and standard deviation σ?	
For the binomial distribution $X \sim B(n, p)$, what is the mean and what is the variance?	
How do you transform the normal distribution $X \sim N(\mu, \sigma^2)$ to the standard normal distribution Z?	
When can you use the normal distribution to approximate the binomial distribution $X \sim B(n, p)$?	
$\sum_{\text{all } x} P(X = x) = ?$	
For the normal distribution $X \sim N(\mu, \sigma^2)$, where are the points of inflection?	
How many ways can n different objects be arranged if r of them are the same?	
Which continuous probability distribution has a symmetrical bell-shaped curve?	

Quiz 14: Statistical distributions

When can you use the normal distribution to approximate the binomial distribution $X \sim B(n, p)$?	
$\sum_{\text{all } x} P(X = x) = ?$	
For the normal distribution $X \sim N(\mu, \sigma^2)$, where are the points of inflection?	
For a normal distribution, how much of the area under the curve lies within 1 standard deviation of the mean?	
How do we denote a normal distribution with mean μ and standard deviation σ?	
For a discrete distribution, what is the cumulative distribution function?	
How many ways can n different objects be arranged if r of them are the same?	
Which continuous probability distribution has a symmetrical bell-shaped curve?	
How do you transform the normal distribution $X \sim N(\mu, \sigma^2)$ to the standard normal distribution Z?	
What is a discrete random variable?	
What does $P(X = x)$ mean?	
For the binomial distribution $X \sim B(n, p)$, what is the mean and what is the variance?	

Quiz 15: Statistical hypothesis testing

ANSWER KEY

15.1	What is a hypothesis?	A statement that you believe to be true
15.2	How do we denote the null hypothesis?	H_0
15.3	What is a "test statistic"?	A statistic that is calculated from a sample and used to decide whether to reject the null hypothesis or not
15.4	What is the significance level of a hypothesis test?	The probability of incorrectly rejecting the null hypothesis
15.5	What is the critical value of a hypothesis test?	The first value inside the critical region. Results as extreme as the critical value will lead to the null hypothesis being rejected
15.6	When carrying out a hypothesis test for a normal distribution, what parameter can your test investigate?	The mean, μ
15.7	What is the null hypothesis?	The null hypothesis is what you believe to be true, in the absence of any data from a sample
15.8	When using a hypothesis test for correlation, what is the null hypothesis?	That there is no correlation between the two variables, i.e. $p = 0$
15.9	What is the difference between a one-tailed hypothesis test and a two-tailed hypothesis test?	A one-tailed test is specific about whether the true value of a quantity is less than or more than the null hypothesis. A two-tailed test is only concerned with whether the true value of a quantity is different to the null hypothesis
15.10	In the context of hypothesis testing, what does H_1 represent?	The alternative hypothesis
15.11	What is the critical region in a hypothesis test?	The set of all values of the test statistic which would lead you to reject the null hypothesis
15.12	Why must you *not* write "We accept the null hypothesis"?	Just because the sample doesn't lead you to reject the null hypothesis, the null hypothesis could in fact still be wrong

Quiz 15: Statistical hypothesis testing

TRACKER

Quiz	Date	Score
1		
2		
3		
4		
5		
6		

Got it? ☐

Quiz 15: Statistical hypothesis testing

15.1	What is a hypothesis?	
15.2	How do we denote the null hypothesis?	
15.3	What is a "test statistic"?	
15.4	What is the significance level of a hypothesis test?	
15.5	What is the critical value of a hypothesis test?	
15.6	When carrying out a hypothesis test for a normal distribution, what parameter can your test investigate?	
15.7	What is the null hypothesis?	
15.8	When using a hypothesis test for correlation, what is the null hypothesis?	
15.9	What is the difference between a one-tailed hypothesis test and a two-tailed hypothesis test?	
15.10	In the context of hypothesis testing, what does H_1 represent?	
15.11	What is the critical region in a hypothesis test?	
15.12	Why must you *not* write "We accept the null hypothesis"?	

Quiz 15: Statistical hypothesis testing

What is a "test statistic"?	
When carrying out a hypothesis test for a normal distribution, what parameter can your test investigate?	
What is the difference between a one-tailed hypothesis test and a two-tailed hypothesis test?	
Why must you *not* write "We accept the null hypothesis"?	
How do we denote the null hypothesis?	
What is the significance level of a hypothesis test?	
When using a hypothesis test for correlation, what is the null hypothesis?	
In the context of hypothesis testing, what does H_1 represent?	
What is a hypothesis?	
What is the critical value of a hypothesis test?	
What is the null hypothesis?	
What is the critical region in a hypothesis test?	

Quiz 15: Statistical hypothesis testing

In the context of hypothesis testing, what does H_1 represent?	
What is a hypothesis?	
What is the critical value of a hypothesis test?	
When carrying out a hypothesis test for a normal distribution, what parameter can your test investigate?	
How do we denote the null hypothesis?	
What is the difference between a one-tailed hypothesis test and a two-tailed hypothesis test?	
What is the null hypothesis?	
What is the critical region in a hypothesis test?	
When using a hypothesis test for correlation, what is the null hypothesis?	
Why must you *not* write "We accept the null hypothesis"?	
What is a "test statistic"?	
What is the significance level of a hypothesis test?	

Quiz 15: Statistical hypothesis testing

When carrying out a hypothesis test for a normal distribution, what parameter can your test investigate?	
Why must you *not* write "We accept the null hypothesis"?	
What is a hypothesis?	
What is a "test statistic"?	
What is the null hypothesis?	
What is the critical value of a hypothesis test?	
What is the critical region in a hypothesis test?	
When using a hypothesis test for correlation, what is the null hypothesis?	
What is the significance level of a hypothesis test?	
In the context of hypothesis testing, what does H_1 represent?	
How do we denote the null hypothesis?	
What is the difference between a one-tailed hypothesis test and a two-tailed hypothesis test?	

Quiz 15: Statistical hypothesis testing

What is a "test statistic"?	
When carrying out a hypothesis test for a normal distribution, what parameter can your test investigate?	
What is the difference between a one-tailed hypothesis test and a two-tailed hypothesis test?	
Why must you *not* write "We accept the null hypothesis"?	
How do we denote the null hypothesis?	
What is the significance level of a hypothesis test?	
When using a hypothesis test for correlation, what is the null hypothesis?	
In the context of hypothesis testing, what does H_1 represent?	
What is a hypothesis?	
What is the critical value of a hypothesis test?	
What is the null hypothesis?	
What is the critical region in a hypothesis test?	

Quiz 15: Statistical hypothesis testing

In the context of hypothesis testing, what does H_1 represent?	
What is a hypothesis?	
What is the critical value of a hypothesis test?	
When carrying out a hypothesis test for a normal distribution, what parameter can your test investigate?	
How do we denote the null hypothesis?	
What is the difference between a one-tailed hypothesis test and a two-tailed hypothesis test?	
What is the null hypothesis?	
What is the critical region in a hypothesis test?	
When using a hypothesis test for correlation, what is the null hypothesis?	
Why must you *not* write "We accept the null hypothesis"?	
What is a "test statistic"?	
What is the significance level of a hypothesis test?	

Quiz 16: Kinematics

ANSWER KEY

16.1	What is the difference between speed and velocity?	Velocity is a vector quantity and so has direction as well as magnitude. Speed is the magnitude of velocity
16.2	In the SUVAT equations, what do the letters stand for?	S – displacement U – initial velocity V – final velocity A – acceleration T – time
16.3	What property allows you to find the maximum height of a projectile?	At the maximum height, the vertical velocity will be 0
16.4	A projectile projected at a speed u at an angle θ to the horizontal. What is the equation for its vertical displacement y, in terms of its horizontal displacement x?	$y = x \tan(\theta) - \dfrac{gx^2}{2u^2 \cos(\theta)}$
16.5	If a particle is projected at an angle θ to the horizontal with speed u, what are the initial horizontal and vertical velocities?	$u_H = u \cos(\theta)$ $u_V = u \sin(\theta)$
16.6	How do you find the distance travelled from a velocity – time graph?	Calculate the area under the graph
16.7	Suppose you have an expression for displacement in terms of time. How can you find an expression for the velocity?	Differentiate with respect to time
16.8	What SUVAT equation allows you to find the final velocity from the initial velocity, acceleration and displacement?	$v^2 = u^2 + 2as$
16.9	Suppose that the velocity of a particle is described as a function of time. How could you find the maximum velocity of this particle?	Differentiate with respect to time, find the stationary point and verify that it is a maximum
16.10	What can be said about the horizontal velocity of a particle undergoing ideal projectile motion?	It doesn't change
16.11	What does the gradient of a line on a displacement – time graph mean?	The gradient is the velocity
16.12	What does "motion under gravity" mean?	It means the particle experiences an acceleration of g towards the centre of the earth in the vertical direction

Quiz 16: Kinematics

TRACKER

Quiz	Date	Score
1		
2		
3		
4		
5		
6		

Got it? ☐

Quiz 16: Kinematics

16.1	What is the difference between speed and velocity?	
16.2	In the SUVAT equations, what do the letters stand for?	
16.3	What property allows you to find the maximum height of a projectile?	
16.4	A projectile projected at a speed u at an angle θ to the horizontal. What is the equation for its vertical displacement y, in terms of its horizontal displacement x?	
16.5	If a particle is projected at an angle θ to the horizontal with speed u, what are the initial horizontal and vertical velocities?	
16.6	How do you find the distance travelled from a velocity – time graph?	
16.7	Suppose you have an expression for displacement in terms of time. How can you find an expression for the velocity?	
16.8	What SUVAT equation allows you to find the final velocity from the initial velocity, acceleration and displacement?	
16.9	Suppose that the velocity of a particle is described as a function of time. How could you find the maximum velocity of this particle?	
16.10	What can be said about the horizontal velocity of a particle undergoing ideal projectile motion?	
16.11	What does the gradient of a line on a displacement – time graph mean?	
16.12	What does "motion under gravity" mean?	

Quiz 16: Kinematics

What property allows you to find the maximum height of a projectile?	
How do you find the distance travelled from a velocity – time graph?	
Suppose that the velocity of a particle is described as a function of time. How could you find the maximum velocity of this particle?	
What does "motion under gravity" mean?	
In the SUVAT equations, what do the letters stand for?	
A projectile projected at a speed u at an angle θ to the horizontal. What is the equation for its vertical displacement y, in terms of its horizontal displacement x?	
What SUVAT equation allows you to find the final velocity from the initial velocity, acceleration and displacement?	
What can be said about the horizontal velocity of a particle undergoing ideal projectile motion?	
What is the difference between speed and velocity?	
If a particle is projected at an angle θ to the horizontal with speed u, what are the initial horizontal and vertical velocities?	
Suppose you have an expression for displacement in terms of time. How can you find an expression for the velocity?	
What does the gradient of a line on a displacement – time graph mean?	

Quiz 16: Kinematics

What can be said about the horizontal velocity of a particle undergoing ideal projectile motion?	
What is the difference between speed and velocity?	
If a particle is projected at an angle θ to the horizontal with speed u, what are the initial horizontal and vertical velocities?	
How do you find the distance travelled from a velocity – time graph?	
In the SUVAT equations, what do the letters stand for?	
Suppose that the velocity of a particle is described as a function of time. How could you find the maximum velocity of this particle?	
Suppose you have an expression for displacement in terms of time. How can you find an expression for the velocity?	
What does the gradient of a line on a displacement – time graph mean?	
What SUVAT equation allows you to find the final velocity from the initial velocity, acceleration and displacement?	
What does "motion under gravity" mean?	
What property allows you to find the maximum height of a projectile?	
A projectile projected at a speed u at an angle θ to the horizontal. What is the equation for its vertical displacement y, in terms of its horizontal displacement x?	

Quiz 16: Kinematics

How do you find the distance travelled from a velocity – time graph?	
What does "motion under gravity" mean?	
What is the difference between speed and velocity?	
What property allows you to find the maximum height of a projectile?	
Suppose you have an expression for displacement in terms of time. How can you find an expression for the velocity?	
If a particle is projected at an angle θ to the horizontal with speed u, what are the initial horizontal and vertical velocities?	
What does the gradient of a line on a displacement – time graph mean?	
What SUVAT equation allows you to find the final velocity from the initial velocity, acceleration and displacement?	
A projectile projected at a speed u at an angle θ to the horizontal. What is the equation for its vertical displacement y, in terms of its horizontal displacement x?	
What can be said about the horizontal velocity of a particle undergoing ideal projectile motion?	
In the SUVAT equations, what do the letters stand for?	
Suppose that the velocity of a particle is described as a function of time. How could you find the maximum velocity of this particle?	

Quiz 16: Kinematics

What property allows you to find the maximum height of a projectile?	
How do you find the distance travelled from a velocity – time graph?	
Suppose that the velocity of a particle is described as a function of time. How could you find the maximum velocity of this particle?	
What does "motion under gravity" mean?	
In the SUVAT equations, what do the letters stand for?	
A projectile projected at a speed u at an angle θ to the horizontal. What is the equation for its vertical displacement y, in terms of its horizontal displacement x?	
What SUVAT equation allows you to find the final velocity from the initial velocity, acceleration and displacement?	
What can be said about the horizontal velocity of a particle undergoing ideal projectile motion?	
What is the difference between speed and velocity?	
If a particle is projected at an angle θ to the horizontal with speed u, what are the initial horizontal and vertical velocities?	
Suppose you have an expression for displacement in terms of time. How can you find an expression for the velocity?	
What does the gradient of a line on a displacement – time graph mean?	

Quiz 16: Kinematics

What can be said about the horizontal velocity of a particle undergoing ideal projectile motion?	
What is the difference between speed and velocity?	
If a particle is projected at an angle θ to the horizontal with speed u, what are the initial horizontal and vertical velocities?	
How do you find the distance travelled from a velocity – time graph?	
In the SUVAT equations, what do the letters stand for?	
Suppose that the velocity of a particle is described as a function of time. How could you find the maximum velocity of this particle?	
Suppose you have an expression for displacement in terms of time. How can you find an expression for the velocity?	
What does the gradient of a line on a displacement – time graph mean?	
What SUVAT equation allows you to find the final velocity from the initial velocity, acceleration and displacement?	
What does "motion under gravity" mean?	
What property allows you to find the maximum height of a projectile?	
A projectile projected at a speed u at an angle θ to the horizontal. What is the equation for its vertical displacement y, in terms of its horizontal displacement x?	

Quiz 17: Forces and Newton's laws

ANSWER KEY

17.1	What does the modelling assumption "uniform" mean?	The mass is evenly distributed throughout the body. Its mass can be taken to act through the body's centre of mass
17.2	When we say a particle is in "equilibrium", what do we mean?	There is no resultant force acting on the particle
17.3	What does Newton's First Law of Motion say?	A body will remain at rest or move at a constant velocity unless a non-zero resultant force acts on it
17.4	What is the weight of a body?	The weight of a body is the product of its mass with the acceleration due to gravity. It is a force and so has units N
17.5	In which direction does friction act?	In the direction opposing motion
17.6	Suppose lots of forces are acting on a particle. How would you find the magnitude and direction of the resultant force?	Resolve all forces into directions that are perpendicular to each other and use, on the resultant force, Pythagoras' Theorem to find the magnitude and trigonometry to find the direction, relative to one of your perpendicular directions
17.7	What is a force of one newton equivalent to?	One newton is the force required to accelerate a body of mass 1 kilogram, 1 metre per second per second
17.8	What does "normal reaction force" mean?	The force due to the reaction from the surface a body sits on. The reaction force is always perpendicular to the surface
17.9	What is the SI unit for mass?	The kilogram (kg)
17.10	How is the overall resultant force felt by a particle connected to the particle's motion?	For the resultant force, F, Newton's Second Law of Motion states that $F = ma$, i.e. the mass multiplied by the particle's acceleration is equal to the resultant force acting on the particle
17.11	If two particles connected by a string lie either side of a pulley, what does the pulley being smooth imply?	The tension in the string either side of the pulley is the same
17.12	How does a friction force depend on the normal reaction?	$F \leq \mu R$, where F is the friction force felt by a body, R is the normal reaction and μ is known as the coefficient of friction

Quiz 17: Forces and Newton's laws

TRACKER

Quiz	Date	Score
1		
2		
3		
4		
5		
6		

Got it? ☐

Quiz 17: Forces and Newton's laws

17.1	What does the modelling assumption "uniform" mean?	
17.2	When we say a particle is in "equilibrium", what do we mean?	
17.3	What does Newton's First Law of Motion say?	
17.4	What is the weight of a body?	
17.5	In which direction does friction act?	
17.6	Suppose lots of forces are acting on a particle. How would you find the magnitude and direction of the resultant force?	
17.7	What is a force of one newton equivalent to?	
17.8	What does "normal reaction force" mean?	
17.9	What is the SI unit for mass?	
17.10	How is the overall resultant force felt by a particle connected to the particle's motion?	
17.11	If two particles connected by a string lie either side of a pulley, what does the pulley being smooth imply?	
17.12	How does a friction force depend on the normal reaction?	

Quiz 17: Forces and Newton's laws

What does Newton's First Law of Motion say?	
Suppose lots of forces are acting on a particle. How would you find the magnitude and direction of the resultant force?	
What is the SI unit for mass?	
What does "normal reaction force" mean?	
When we say a particle is in "equilibrium", what do we mean?	
What is the weight of a body?	
How does a friction force depend on the normal reaction?	
How is the overall resultant force felt by a particle connected to the particle's motion?	
What does the modelling assumption "uniform" mean?	
In which direction does friction act?	
What is a force of one newton equivalent to?	
If two particles connected by a string lie either side of a pulley, what does the pulley being smooth imply?	

Quiz 17: Forces and Newton's laws

How is the overall resultant force felt by a particle connected to the particle's motion?	
What does the modelling assumption "uniform" mean?	
In which direction does friction act?	
Suppose lots of forces are acting on a particle. How would you find the magnitude and direction of the resultant force?	
When we say a particle is in "equilibrium", what do we mean?	
What is the SI unit for mass?	
What is a force of one newton equivalent to?	
If two particles connected by a string lie either side of a pulley, what does the pulley being smooth imply?	
How does a friction force depend on the normal reaction?	
What does "normal reaction force" mean?	
What does Newton's First Law of Motion say?	
What is the weight of a body?	

Quiz 17: Forces and Newton's laws

Suppose lots of forces are acting on a particle. How would you find the magnitude and direction of the resultant force?	
What does "normal reaction force" mean?	
What does the modelling assumption "uniform" mean?	
What does Newton's First Law of Motion say?	
What is a force of one newton equivalent to?	
In which direction does friction act?	
If two particles connected by a string lie either side of a pulley, what does the pulley being smooth imply?	
How does a friction force depend on the normal reaction?	
What is the weight of a body?	
How is the overall resultant force felt by a particle connected to the particle's motion?	
When we say a particle is in "equilibrium", what do we mean?	
What is the SI unit for mass?	

Quiz 17: Forces and Newton's laws

What does Newton's First Law of Motion say?	
Suppose lots of forces are acting on a particle. How would you find the magnitude and direction of the resultant force?	
What is the SI unit for mass?	
What does "normal reaction force" mean?	
When we say a particle is in "equilibrium", what do we mean?	
What is the weight of a body?	
How does a friction force depend on the normal reaction?	
How is the overall resultant force felt by a particle connected to the particle's motion?	
What does the modelling assumption "uniform" mean?	
In which direction does friction act?	
What is a force of one newton equivalent to?	
If two particles connected by a string lie either side of a pulley, what does the pulley being smooth imply?	

Quiz 17: Forces and Newton's laws

How is the overall resultant force felt by a particle connected to the particle's motion?	
What does the modelling assumption "uniform" mean?	
In which direction does friction act?	
Suppose lots of forces are acting on a particle. How would you find the magnitude and direction of the resultant force?	
When we say a particle is in "equilibrium", what do we mean?	
What is the SI unit for mass?	
What is a force of one newton equivalent to?	
If two particles connected by a string lie either side of a pulley, what does the pulley being smooth imply?	
How does a friction force depend on the normal reaction?	
What does "normal reaction force" mean?	
What does Newton's First Law of Motion say?	
What is the weight of a body?	

Quiz 18: Moments

ANSWER KEY

18.1	If a system is in equilibrium, what does this mean about the moments about a given point?	The anticlockwise moment about the given point is equal to the clockwise moment about the given point
18.2	The anticlockwise moment of a body about a given point is greater than the clockwise moment about that point. In which direction will the body turn?	Anticlockwise
18.3	What is a "moment"?	A moment is the turning effect of a force about a particular point
18.4	A force of 3N acts at a perpendicular distance of 2m from the point A. What is the moment about A?	6Nm
18.5	How do you calculate the moment of a force, F, about a point A?	Let d be the perpendicular distance from the point A to the line of action of the force F. Then moment about $A = F \times d$
18.6	A uniform rod is suspended by two inextensible wires connected at the ends of the rod. Where would the weight of the rod act through?	The centre of the rod
18.7	If a rod is connected to a fixed horizontal or vertical surface with a hinge, how would you represent the reaction at the surface on a force diagram?	As having both a vertical and horizontal component
18.8	If a shape is described as a lamina, what does this mean about the object?	The thickness of the shape can be ignored, i.e. it can be modelled as two dimensional
18.9	What are the units of a moment?	Nm
18.10	What is meant when a rod resting on a support at A is said to be on the point of tilting at A?	The reaction force at A is equal to zero
18.11	Suppose an inclined rod is resting on a peg. What do we know about the reaction of the rod to the peg?	The reaction force at the peg is perpendicular to the rod
18.12	Suppose a plank is resting on two supports at A and B. What force is felt by the plank at the supports?	A normal reaction force

Quiz 18: Moments

TRACKER

Quiz	Date	Score
1		
2		
3		
4		
5		
6		

Got it? ☐

Quiz 18: Moments

18.1	If a system is in equilibrium, what does this mean about the moments about a given point?	
18.2	The anticlockwise moment of a body about a given point is greater than the clockwise moment about that point. In which direction will the body turn?	
18.3	What is a "moment"?	
18.4	A force of 3N acts at a perpendicular distance of 2m from the point A. What is the moment about A?	
18.5	How do you calculate the moment of a force, F, about a point A?	
18.6	A uniform rod is suspended by two inextensible wires connected at the ends of the rod. Where would the weight of the rod act through?	
18.7	If a rod is connected to a fixed horizontal or vertical surface with a hinge, how would you represent the reaction at the surface on a force diagram?	
18.8	If a shape is described as a lamina, what does this mean about the object?	
18.9	What are the units of a moment?	
18.10	What is meant when a rod resting on a support at A is said to be on the point of tilting at A?	
18.11	Suppose an inclined rod is resting on a peg. What do we know about the reaction of the rod to the peg?	
18.12	Suppose a plank is resting on two supports at A and B. What force is felt by the plank at the supports?	

Quiz 18: Moments

What is a "moment"?	
A uniform rod is suspended by two inextensible wires connected at the ends of the rod. Where would the weight of the rod act through?	
What are the units of a moment?	
Suppose a plank is resting on two supports at A and B. What force is felt by the plank at the supports?	
The anticlockwise moment of a body about a given point is greater than the clockwise moment about that point. In which direction will the body turn?	
A force of 3N acts at a perpendicular distance of 2m from the point A. What is the moment about A?	
If a shape is described as a lamina, what does this mean about the object?	
What is meant when a rod resting on a support at A is said to be on the point of tilting at A?	
If a system is in equilibrium, what does this mean about the moments about a given point?	
How do you calculate the moment of a force, F, about a point A?	
If a rod is connected to a fixed horizontal or vertical surface with a hinge, how would you represent the reaction at the surface on a force diagram?	
Suppose an inclined rod is resting on a peg. What do we know about the reaction of the rod to the peg?	

Quiz 18: Moments

What is meant when a rod resting on a support at A is said to be on the point of tilting at A?	
If a system is in equilibrium, what does this mean about the moments about a given point?	
How do you calculate the moment of a force, F, about a point A?	
A uniform rod is suspended by two inextensible wires connected at the ends of the rod. Where would the weight of the rod act through?	
The anticlockwise moment of a body about a given point is greater than the clockwise moment about that point. In which direction will the body turn?	
What are the units of a moment?	
If a rod is connected to a fixed horizontal or vertical surface with a hinge, how would you represent the reaction at the surface on a force diagram?	
Suppose an inclined rod is resting on a peg. What do we know about the reaction of the rod to the peg?	
If a shape is described as a lamina, what does this mean about the object?	
Suppose a plank is resting on two supports at A and B. What force is felt by the plank at the supports?	
What is a "moment"?	
A force of 3N acts at a perpendicular distance of 2m from the point A. What is the moment about A?	

Quiz 18: Moments

A uniform rod is suspended by two inextensible wires connected at the ends of the rod. Where would the weight of the rod act through?	
Suppose a plank is resting on two supports at A and B. What force is felt by the plank at the supports?	
If a system is in equilibrium, what does this mean about the moments about a given point?	
What is a "moment"?	
If a rod is connected to a fixed horizontal or vertical surface with a hinge, how would you represent the reaction at the surface on a force diagram?	
How do you calculate the moment of a force, F, about a point A?	
Suppose an inclined rod is resting on a peg. What do we know about the reaction of the rod to the peg?	
If a shape is described as a lamina, what does this mean about the object?	
A force of 3N acts at a perpendicular distance of 2m from the point A. What is the moment about A?	
What is meant when a rod resting on a support at A is said to be on the point of tilting at A?	
The anticlockwise moment of a body about a given point is greater than the clockwise moment about that point. In which direction will the body turn?	
What are the units of a moment?	

Quiz 18: Moments

What is a "moment"?	
A uniform rod is suspended by two inextensible wires connected at the ends of the rod. Where would the weight of the rod act through?	
What are the units of a moment?	
Suppose a plank is resting on two supports at A and B. What force is felt by the plank at the supports?	
The anticlockwise moment of a body about a given point is greater than the clockwise moment about that point. In which direction will the body turn?	
A force of 3N acts at a perpendicular distance of 2m from the point A. What is the moment about A?	
If a shape is described as a lamina, what does this mean about the object?	
What is meant when a rod resting on a support at A is said to be on the point of tilting at A?	
If a system is in equilibrium, what does this mean about the moments about a given point?	
How do you calculate the moment of a force, F, about a point A?	
If a rod is connected to a fixed horizontal or vertical surface with a hinge, how would you represent the reaction at the surface on a force diagram?	
Suppose an inclined rod is resting on a peg. What do we know about the reaction of the rod to the peg?	

Quiz 18: Moments

What is meant when a rod resting on a support at A is said to be on the point of tilting at A?	
If a system is in equilibrium, what does this mean about the moments about a given point?	
How do you calculate the moment of a force, F, about a point A?	
A uniform rod is suspended by two inextensible wires connected at the ends of the rod. Where would the weight of the rod act through?	
The anticlockwise moment of a body about a given point is greater than the clockwise moment about that point. In which direction will the body turn?	
What are the units of a moment?	
If a rod is connected to a fixed horizontal or vertical surface with a hinge, how would you represent the reaction at the surface on a force diagram?	
Suppose an inclined rod is resting on a peg. What do we know about the reaction of the rod to the peg?	
If a shape is described as a lamina, what does this mean about the object?	
Suppose a plank is resting on two supports at A and B. What force is felt by the plank at the supports?	
What is a "moment"?	
A force of 3N acts at a perpendicular distance of 2m from the point A. What is the moment about A?	

Revision

Quiz R1: Revision 1

ANSWER KEY

R1.1	State the factor theorem	If $f\left(\dfrac{b}{a}\right) = 0$ then $(ax - b)$ is a factor of $f(x)$
R1.2	Describe how you could find the turning point of the quadratic $y = ax^2 + bx + c$ by completing the square	Write in the form $a\left(x + \dfrac{b}{2a}\right)^2 + \left(c - \dfrac{b^2}{4a}\right)$ and then the turning point has coordinate $\left(-\dfrac{b}{2a}, c - \dfrac{b^2}{4a}\right)$
R1.3	A tangent to a circle meets the radius at...	$90°$
R1.4	Complete the logarithm law: $\log_c(a) + \log_c(b) =$	$\log_c(a) + \log_c(b) = \log_c(ab)$
R1.5	$\int \tan(x)\, dx =$	$\int \tan(x)\, dx = -\ln|\cos(x)| + C$
R1.6	The gradient of the straight line through the points $A(x_A, y_A)$ and $B(x_B, y_B)$ is...	$\dfrac{y_B - y_A}{x_B - x_A}$
R1.7	$\dfrac{d}{dx}\cos(x) =$	$-\sin(x)$
R1.8	The centre of the circle $(x - a)^2 + (y - b)^2 = r^2$ is...	(a, b)
R1.9	What does the term "light and inextensible" mean?	The object has no mass and cannot be stretched
R1.10	What does Newton's First Law of Motion say?	A body will remain at rest or move at a constant velocity unless a non-zero resultant force acts on it
R1.11	Define the term "systematic sampling"	Every nth member of a population is selected
R1.12	When can you use the normal distribution to approximate the binomial distribution $X \sim B(n,p)$?	If n is large and $p \approx 0.5$

Quiz R1: Revision 1

TRACKER

Quiz	Date	Score
1		
2		
3		
4		
5		
6		

Got it? ☐

Quiz R1: Revision 1

R1.1	State the factor theorem	
R1.2	Describe how you could find the turning point of the quadratic $y = ax^2 + bx + c$ by completing the square	
R1.3	A tangent to a circle meets the radius at...	
R1.4	Complete the logarithm law: $\log_c(a) + \log_c(b) =$	
R1.5	$\int \tan(x)\, dx =$	
R1.6	The gradient of the straight line through the points $A(x_A, y_A)$ and $B(x_B, y_B)$ is...	
R1.7	$\dfrac{d}{dx}\cos(x) =$	
R1.8	The centre of the circle $(x - a)^2 + (y - b)^2 = r^2$ is...	
R1.9	What does the term "light and inextensible" mean?	
R1.10	What does Newton's First Law of Motion say?	
R1.11	Define the term "systematic sampling"	
R1.12	When can you use the normal distribution to approximate the binomial distribution $X \sim B(n,p)$?	

Quiz R1: Revision 1

A tangent to a circle meets the radius at...	
The gradient of the straight line through the points $A(x_A, y_A)$ and $B(x_B, y_B)$ is...	
What does the term "light and inextensible" mean?	
When can you use the normal distribution to approximate the binomial distribution $X \sim B(n,p)$?	
Describe how you could find the turning point of the quadratic $y = ax^2 + bx + c$ by completing the square	
Complete the logarithm law: $\log_c(a) + \log_c(b) =$	
The centre of the circle $(x - a)^2 + (y - b)^2 = r^2$ is...	
What does Newton's First Law of Motion say?	
State the factor theorem	
$\int \tan(x) \, dx =$	
$\dfrac{d}{dx} \cos(x) =$	
Define the term "systematic sampling"	

Quiz R1: Revision 1

What does Newton's First Law of Motion say?	
State the factor theorem	
$\int \tan(x)\, dx =$	
The gradient of the straight line through the points $A(x_A, y_A)$ and $B(x_B, y_B)$ is...	
Describe how you could find the turning point of the quadratic $y = ax^2 + bx + c$ by completing the square	
What does the term "light and inextensible" mean?	
$\dfrac{d}{dx} \cos(x) =$	
Define the term "systematic sampling"	
The centre of the circle $(x - a)^2 + (y - b)^2 = r^2$ is...	
When can you use the normal distribution to approximate the binomial distribution $X \sim B(n,p)$?	
A tangent to a circle meets the radius at...	
Complete the logarithm law: $\log_c(a) + \log_c(b) =$	

Quiz R1: Revision 1

The gradient of the straight line through the points $A(x_A, y_A)$ and $B(x_B, y_B)$ is...	
When can you use the normal distribution to approximate the binomial distribution $X \sim B(n,p)$?	
State the factor theorem	
A tangent to a circle meets the radius at...	
$\dfrac{d}{dx} \cos(x) =$	
$\int \tan(x) \, dx =$	
Define the term "systematic sampling"	
The centre of the circle $(x - a)^2 + (y - b)^2 = r^2$ is...	
Complete the logarithm law: $\log_c(a) + \log_c(b) =$	
What does Newton's First Law of Motion say?	
Describe how you could find the turning point of the quadratic $y = ax^2 + bx + c$ by completing the square	
What does the term "light and inextensible" mean?	

Quiz R1: Revision 1

A tangent to a circle meets the radius at...	
The gradient of the straight line through the points $A(x_A, y_A)$ and $B(x_B, y_B)$ is...	
What does the term "light and inextensible" mean?	
When can you use the normal distribution to approximate the binomial distribution $X \sim B(n,p)$?	
Describe how you could find the turning point of the quadratic $y = ax^2 + bx + c$ by completing the square	
Complete the logarithm law: $\log_c(a) + \log_c(b) =$	
The centre of the circle $(x - a)^2 + (y - b)^2 = r^2$ is...	
What does Newton's First Law of Motion say?	
State the factor theorem	
$\int \tan(x) \, dx =$	
$\dfrac{d}{dx} \cos(x) =$	
Define the term "systematic sampling"	

Quiz R1: Revision 1

What does Newton's First Law of Motion say?	
State the factor theorem	
$\int \tan(x) \, dx =$	
The gradient of the straight line through the points $A(x_A, y_A)$ and $B(x_B, y_B)$ is...	
Describe how you could find the turning point of the quadratic $y = ax^2 + bx + c$ by completing the square	
What does the term "light and inextensible" mean?	
$\dfrac{d}{dx} \cos(x) =$	
Define the term "systematic sampling"	
The centre of the circle $(x - a)^2 + (y - b)^2 = r^2$ is...	
When can you use the normal distribution to approximate the binomial distribution $X \sim B(n,p)$?	
A tangent to a circle meets the radius at...	
Complete the logarithm law: $\log_c(a) + \log_c(b) =$	

Quiz R2: Revision 2

ANSWER KEY

R2.1	For fractional n, under what conditions is the binomial expansion $(1+x)^n$ valid?	$\|x\| < 1$
R2.2	The distance between the points $A(x_A, y_A, z_A)$ and $B(x_B, y_B, z_B)$ is...	$\sqrt{(x_B-x_A)^2 + (y_B-y_A)^2 + (z_B-z_A)^2}$
R2.3	State the quadratic formula for the quadratic $ax^2 + bx + cx = 0$	$x = \dfrac{-b \pm \sqrt{b^2-4ac}}{2a}$
R2.4	Complete the logarithm law: $\log_c(a) - \log_c(b) =$	$\log_c(a) - \log_c(b) = \log_c\left(\dfrac{a}{b}\right)$
R2.5	$\dfrac{d}{dx}\ln(x) =$	$\dfrac{1}{x}$
R2.6	For $a \in \mathbb{R}$, $\displaystyle\int a^x \, dx =$	$a^x \ln\|a\| + C$
R2.7	State the quotient rule for differentiating $y = \dfrac{u(x)}{v(x)}$	$\dfrac{dy}{dx} = \dfrac{v\frac{du}{dx} - u\frac{dv}{dx}}{v^2}$
R2.8	State the trigonometric Pythagorean identities	$\cos^2(x) + \sin^2(x) \equiv 1$ $1 + \tan^2(x) \equiv \sec^2(x)$ $1 + \cot^2(x) \equiv \operatorname{cosec}^2(x)$
R2.9	Define the term "moment"	A moment is the turning effect of a force about a particular point
R2.10	What does it mean for a system to be in equilibrium?	There is no resultant force acting on the particle
R2.11	What is the standard deviation of a set of data a measure of?	A measure of how spread out the data is from the mean
R2.12	How do you standardise a normal distribution $X \sim N(\mu, \sigma^2)$?	$Z \sim \dfrac{X-\mu}{\sigma}$ where $Z \sim N(0,1)$

Quiz R2: Revision 2

TRACKER

Quiz	Date	Score
1		
2		
3		
4		
5		
6		

Got it? ☐

Quiz R2: Revision 2

R2.1	For fractional n, under what conditions is the binomial expansion $(1+x)^n$ valid?	
R2.2	The distance between the points $A(x_A, y_A, z_A)$ and $B(x_B, y_B, z_B)$ is...	
R2.3	State the quadratic formula for the quadratic $ax^2 + bx + cx = 0$	
R2.4	Complete the logarithm law: $\log_c(a) - \log_c(b) =$	
R2.5	$\dfrac{d}{dx}\ln(x) =$	
R2.6	For $a \in \mathbb{R}$, $\int a^x \, dx =$	
R2.7	State the quotient rule for differentiating $y = \dfrac{u(x)}{v(x)}$	
R2.8	State the trigonometric Pythagorean identities	
R2.9	Define the term "moment"	
R2.10	What does it mean for a system to be in equilibrium?	
R2.11	What is the standard deviation of a set of data a measure of?	
R2.12	How do you standardise a normal distribution $X \sim N(\mu, \sigma^2)$?	

Quiz R2: Revision 2

State the quadratic formula for the quadratic $ax^2 + bx + cx = 0$	
For $a \in \mathbb{R}$, $\int a^x \, dx =$	
Define the term "moment"	
How do you standardise a normal distribution $X \sim N(\mu, \sigma^2)$?	
The distance between the points $A(x_A, y_A, z_A)$ and $B(x_B, y_B, z_B)$ is...	
Complete the logarithm law: $\log_c(a) - \log_c(b) =$	
State the trigonometric Pythagorean identities	
What does it mean for a system to be in equilibrium?	
For fractional n, under what conditions is the binomial expansion $(1 + x)^n$ valid?	
$\dfrac{d}{dx} \ln(x) =$	
State the quotient rule for differentiating $y = \dfrac{u(x)}{v(x)}$	
What is the standard deviation of a set of data a measure of?	

Quiz R2: Revision 2

What does it mean for a system to be in equilibrium?	
For fractional n, under what conditions is the binomial expansion $(1 + x)^n$ valid?	
$\dfrac{d}{dx} \ln(x) =$	
For $a \in \mathbb{R}$, $\displaystyle\int a^x \, dx =$	
The distance between the points $A(x_A, y_A, z_A)$ and $B(x_B, y_B, z_B)$ is...	
Define the term "moment"	
State the quotient rule for differentiating $y = \dfrac{u(x)}{v(x)}$	
What is the standard deviation of a set of data a measure of?	
State the trigonometric Pythagorean identities	
How do you standardise a normal distribution $X \sim N(\mu, \sigma^2)$?	
State the quadratic formula for the quadratic $ax^2 + bx + cx = 0$	
Complete the logarithm law: $\log_c(a) - \log_c(b) =$	

Quiz R2: Revision 2

For $a \in \mathbb{R}$, $\int a^x \, dx =$	
How do you standardise a normal distribution $X \sim N(\mu, \sigma^2)$?	
For fractional n, under what conditions is the binomial expansion $(1 + x)^n$ valid?	
State the quadratic formula for the quadratic $ax^2 + bx + cx = 0$	
State the quotient rule for differentiating $y = \dfrac{u(x)}{v(x)}$	
$\dfrac{d}{dx} \ln(x) =$	
What is the standard deviation of a set of data a measure of?	
State the trigonometric Pythagorean identities	
Complete the logarithm law: $\log_c(a) - \log_c(b) =$	
What does it mean for a system to be in equilibrium?	
The distance between the points $A(x_A, y_A, z_A)$ and $B(x_B, y_B, z_B)$ is...	
Define the term "moment"	

Quiz R2: Revision 2

State the quadratic formula for the quadratic $ax^2 + bx + cx = 0$	
For $a \in \mathbb{R}$, $\int a^x \, dx =$	
Define the term "moment"	
How do you standardise a normal distribution $X \sim N(\mu, \sigma^2)$?	
The distance between the points $A(x_A, y_A, z_A)$ and $B(x_B, y_B, z_B)$ is...	
Complete the logarithm law: $\log_c(a) - \log_c(b) =$	
State the trigonometric Pythagorean identities	
What does it mean for a system to be in equilibrium?	
For fractional n, under what conditions is the binomial expansion $(1+x)^n$ valid?	
$\dfrac{d}{dx} \ln(x) =$	
State the quotient rule for differentiating $y = \dfrac{u(x)}{v(x)}$	
What is the standard deviation of a set of data a measure of?	

Quiz R2: Revision 2

What does it mean for a system to be in equilibrium?	
For fractional n, under what conditions is the binomial expansion $(1+x)^n$ valid?	
$\dfrac{d}{dx}\ln(x) =$	
For $a \in \mathbb{R}$, $\displaystyle\int a^x \, dx =$	
The distance between the points $A(x_A, y_A, z_A)$ and $B(x_B, y_B, z_B)$ is...	
Define the term "moment"	
State the quotient rule for differentiating $y = \dfrac{u(x)}{v(x)}$	
What is the standard deviation of a set of data a measure of?	
State the trigonometric Pythagorean identities	
How do you standardise a normal distribution $X \sim N(\mu, \sigma^2)$?	
State the quadratic formula for the quadratic $ax^2 + bx + cx = 0$	
Complete the logarithm law: $\log_c(a) - \log_c(b) =$	

Quiz R3: Revision 3

ANSWER KEY

R3.1	State the product rule for differentiation for the functions $y(x) = u(x)v(x)$	$\dfrac{dy}{dx} = u\dfrac{dv}{dx} + v\dfrac{du}{dx}$
R3.2	What is the condition for x_1 to be a non-stationary point of inflection of the function $f(x)$?	$f''(x_1) = 0$
R3.3	Complete the trigonometric identity $\cos(2\theta) =$	$\cos(2\theta) = \cos^2(\theta) - \sin^2(\theta)$ $\cos(2\theta) = 2\cos^2(\theta) - 1$ $\cos(2\theta) = 1 - 2\sin^2(\theta)$
R3.4	How would you evaluate $\int \ln(x)\,dx$?	Integration by parts with $u = \ln(x)$ and $v' = 1$
R3.5	State the cosine rule for a non-right-angled triangle $A\,B\,C$ with corresponding sides a, b and c	$a^2 = b^2 + c^2 - 2bc\cos(A)$
R3.6	For the quadratic $ax^2 + bx + c$, if $b^2 - 4ac = 0$ then...	There are two real repeated roots
R3.7	$y = ax^n \Rightarrow \ln(y) =$	$\ln(y) = n\ln(x) + \ln(a)$
R3.8	How do you determine if a stationary point of a function is a maximum?	The second derivative of the function evaluated at the stationary point is negative
R3.9	Describe the force of tension	A pulling force
R3.10	For non-constant acceleration, how are velocity, v, and displacement, s, linked?	$v = \dfrac{ds}{dt}$
R3.11	What is a dot plot?	Like a bar chart, but where each exact individual piece of data is represented as a dot
R3.12	State the 5 key steps to completing a hypothesis test	State the null and alternative hypothesis; decide on the appropriate test statistics; determine the significance level of the test; compute the value of the test statistic; and then make a conclusion in context

Quiz R3: Revision 3

TRACKER

Quiz	Date	Score
1		
2		
3		
4		
5		
6		

Got it? ☐

Quiz R3: Revision 3

R3.1	State the product rule for differentiation for the functions $y(x) = u(x)v(x)$	
R3.2	What is the condition for x_1 to be a non-stationary point of inflection of the function $f(x)$?	
R3.3	Complete the trigonometric identity $\cos(2\theta) =$	
R3.4	How would you evaluate $\int \ln(x) \, dx$?	
R3.5	State the cosine rule for a non-right-angled triangle $A\ B\ C$ with corresponding sides a, b and c	
R3.6	For the quadratic $ax^2 + bx + c$, if $b^2 - 4ac = 0$ then...	
R3.7	$y = ax^n \Rightarrow \ln(y) =$	
R3.8	How do you determine if a stationary point of a function is a maximum?	
R3.9	Describe the force of tension	
R3.10	For non-constant acceleration, how are velocity, v, and displacement, s, linked?	
R3.11	What is a dot plot?	
R3.12	State the 5 key steps to completing a hypothesis test	

Quiz R3: Revision 3

Complete the trigonometric identity $\cos(2\theta) =$	
For the quadratic $ax^2 + bx + c$, if $b^2 - 4ac = 0$ then...	
Describe the force of tension	
State the 5 key steps to completing a hypothesis test	
What is the condition for x_1 to be a non-stationary point of inflection of the function $f(x)$?	
How would you evaluate $\int \ln(x) \, dx$?	
How do you determine if a stationary point of a function is a maximum?	
For non-constant acceleration, how are velocity, v, and displacement, s, linked?	
State the product rule for differentiation for the functions $y(x) = u(x)v(x)$	
State the cosine rule for a non-right-angled triangle $A\,B\,C$ with corresponding sides a, b and c	
$y = ax^n \Rightarrow \ln(y) =$	
What is a dot plot?	

Quiz R3: Revision 3

For non-constant acceleration, how are velocity, v, and displacement, s, linked?	
State the product rule for differentiation for the functions $y(x) = u(x)v(x)$	
State the cosine rule for a non-right-angled triangle ABC with corresponding sides a, b and c	
For the quadratic $ax^2 + bx + c$, if $b^2 - 4ac = 0$ then...	
What is the condition for x_1 to be a non-stationary point of inflection of the function $f(x)$?	
Describe the force of tension	
$y = ax^n \Rightarrow \ln(y) =$	
What is a dot plot?	
How do you determine if a stationary point of a function is a maximum?	
State the 5 key steps to completing a hypothesis test	
Complete the trigonometric identity $\cos(2\theta) =$	
How would you evaluate $\int \ln(x)\,dx$?	

Quiz R3: Revision 3

For the quadratic $ax^2 + bx + c$, if $b^2 - 4ac = 0$ then...	
State the 5 key steps to completing a hypothesis test	
State the product rule for differentiation for the functions $y(x) = u(x)v(x)$	
Complete the trigonometric identity $\cos(2\theta) =$	
$y = ax^n \Rightarrow \ln(y) =$	
State the cosine rule for a non-right-angled triangle $A\ B\ C$ with corresponding sides a, b and c	
What is a dot plot?	
How do you determine if a stationary point of a function is a maximum?	
How would you evaluate $\int \ln(x)\ dx$?	
For non-constant acceleration, how are velocity, v, and displacement, s, linked?	
What is the condition for x_1 to be a non-stationary point of inflection of the function $f(x)$?	
Describe the force of tension	

Quiz R3: Revision 3

Complete the trigonometric identity $\cos(2\theta) =$	
For the quadratic $ax^2 + bx + c$, if $b^2 - 4ac = 0$ then...	
Describe the force of tension	
State the 5 key steps to completing a hypothesis test	
What is the condition for x_1 to be a non-stationary point of inflection of the function $f(x)$?	
How would you evaluate $\int \ln(x)\,dx$?	
How do you determine if a stationary point of a function is a maximum?	
For non-constant acceleration, how are velocity, v, and displacement, s, linked?	
State the product rule for differentiation for the functions $y(x) = u(x)v(x)$	
State the cosine rule for a non-right-angled triangle $A\,B\,C$ with corresponding sides a, b and c	
$y = ax^n \Rightarrow \ln(y) =$	
What is a dot plot?	

Quiz R3: Revision 3

For non-constant acceleration, how are velocity, v, and displacement, s, linked?	
State the product rule for differentiation for the functions $y(x) = u(x)v(x)$	
State the cosine rule for a non-right-angled triangle ABC with corresponding sides a, b and c	
For the quadratic $ax^2 + bx + c$, if $b^2 - 4ac = 0$ then…	
What is the condition for x_1 to be a non-stationary point of inflection of the function $f(x)$?	
Describe the force of tension	
$y = ax^n \Rightarrow \ln(y) =$	
What is a dot plot?	
How do you determine if a stationary point of a function is a maximum?	
State the 5 key steps to completing a hypothesis test	
Complete the trigonometric identity $\cos(2\theta) =$	
How would you evaluate $\int \ln(x)\, dx$?	

Quiz R4: Revision 4

ANSWER KEY

R4.1	What is the formula for the general term of an arithmetic sequence?	$a + (n - 1)d$ where a is the first term and d is the common difference
R4.2	For the quadratic $ax^2 + bx + c$, if $b^2 - 4ac > 0$ then...	There are two real roots
R4.3	How do you determine if a stationary point of a function is a minimum?	The second derivative of the function evaluated at the stationary point is positive
R4.4	Sketch the graphs $y = \sin(x)$ and $y = \sin(3x)$	*(graph showing both sine curves)*
R4.5	How is the graph of $f^{-1}(x)$ related to the graph of $f(x)$?	They are reflections of each other in the line $y = x$
R4.6	For small θ, state the small-angle approximations for $\sin(\theta)$ and $\cos(\theta)$	$\sin(\theta) \approx \theta$ and $\cos(\theta) \approx 1 - \dfrac{\theta^2}{2}$
R4.7	$\displaystyle\int \dfrac{f'(x)}{f(x)}\, dx =$	$\ln\|f(x)\| + C$
R4.8	$36x^2 - 49$ is an example of...	A difference of two squares
R4.9	How do you find the vertical and horizontal components of a force?	If θ is the angle between the force and the horizontal, then $F_{\text{vert}} = F\sin(\theta)$ and $F_{\text{horiz}} = F\cos(\theta)$
R4.10	A body is trying to slide down an inclined plane. In what direction is the force of friction acting?	Up the plane, to oppose motion
R4.11	Complete the probability rule $P(A \cup B) =$	$P(A \cup B) = P(A) + P(B) - P(A \cap B)$
R4.12	What are the four conditions for a binomial distribution to be a valid model of a situation?	1. A fixed number of trials 2. Each trial is either success or failure 3. The trials are all independent 4. The probability of success is constant

Quiz R4: Revision 4

TRACKER

Quiz	Date	Score
1		
2		
3		
4		
5		
6		

Got it? ☐

Quiz R4: Revision 4

R4.1	What is the formula for the general term of an arithmetic sequence?	
R4.2	For the quadratic $ax^2 + bx + c$, if $b^2 - 4ac > 0$ then...	
R4.3	How do you determine if a stationary point of a function is a minimum?	
R4.4	Sketch the graphs $y = \sin(x)$ and $y = \sin(3x)$	
R4.5	How is the graph of $f^{-1}(x)$ related to the graph of $f(x)$?	
R4.6	For small θ, state the small-angle approximations for $\sin(\theta)$ and $\cos(\theta)$	
R4.7	$\int \dfrac{f'(x)}{f(x)} \, dx =$	
R4.8	$36x^2 - 49$ is an example of...	
R4.9	How do you find the vertical and horizontal components of a force?	
R4.10	A body is trying to slide down an inclined plane. In what direction is the force of friction acting?	
R4.11	Complete the probability rule $P(A \cup B) =$	
R4.12	What are the four conditions for a binomial distribution to be a valid model of a situation?	

Quiz R4: Revision 4

How do you determine if a stationary point of a function is a minimum?	
For small θ, state the small-angle approximations for $\sin(\theta)$ and $\cos(\theta)$	
How do you find the vertical and horizontal components of a force?	
What are the four conditions for a binomial distribution to be a valid model of a situation?	
For the quadratic $ax^2 + bx + c$, if $b^2 - 4ac > 0$ then...	
Sketch the graphs $y = \sin(x)$ and $y = \sin(3x)$	
$36x^2 - 49$ is an example of...	
A body is trying to slide down an inclined plane. In what direction is the force of friction acting?	
What is the formula for the general term of an arithmetic sequence?	
How is the graph of $f^{-1}(x)$ related to the graph of $f(x)$?	
$\int \dfrac{f'(x)}{f(x)} \, dx =$	
Complete the probability rule $P(A \cup B) =$	

Quiz R4: Revision 4

A body is trying to slide down an inclined plane. In what direction is the force of friction acting?	
What is the formula for the general term of an arithmetic sequence?	
How is the graph of $f^{-1}(x)$ related to the graph of $f(x)$?	
For small θ, state the small-angle approximations for $\sin(\theta)$ and $\cos(\theta)$	
For the quadratic $ax^2 + bx + c$, if $b^2 - 4ac > 0$ then...	
How do you find the vertical and horizontal components of a force?	
$\int \frac{f'(x)}{f(x)} \, dx =$	
Complete the probability rule $P(A \cup B) =$	
$36x^2 - 49$ is an example of...	
What are the four conditions for a binomial distribution to be a valid model of a situation?	
How do you determine if a stationary point of a function is a minimum?	
Sketch the graphs $y = \sin(x)$ and $y = \sin(3x)$	

Quiz R4: Revision 4

For small θ, state the small-angle approximations for $\sin(\theta)$ and $\cos(\theta)$	
What are the four conditions for a binomial distribution to be a valid model of a situation?	
What is the formula for the general term of an arithmetic sequence?	
How do you determine if a stationary point of a function is a minimum?	
$\int \dfrac{f'(x)}{f(x)} \, dx =$	
How is the graph of $f^{-1}(x)$ related to the graph of $f(x)$?	
Complete the probability rule $P(A \cup B) =$	
$36x^2 - 49$ is an example of...	
Sketch the graphs $y = \sin(x)$ and $y = \sin(3x)$	
A body is trying to slide down an inclined plane. In what direction is the force of friction acting?	
For the quadratic $ax^2 + bx + c$, if $b^2 - 4ac > 0$ then...	
How do you find the vertical and horizontal components of a force?	

Quiz R4: Revision 4

How do you determine if a stationary point of a function is a minimum?	
For small θ, state the small-angle approximations for $\sin(\theta)$ and $\cos(\theta)$	
How do you find the vertical and horizontal components of a force?	
What are the four conditions for a binomial distribution to be a valid model of a situation?	
For the quadratic $ax^2 + bx + c$, if $b^2 - 4ac > 0$ then...	
Sketch the graphs $y = \sin(x)$ and $y = \sin(3x)$	
$36x^2 - 49$ is an example of...	
A body is trying to slide down an inclined plane. In what direction is the force of friction acting?	
What is the formula for the general term of an arithmetic sequence?	
How is the graph of $f^{-1}(x)$ related to the graph of $f(x)$?	
$\int \dfrac{f'(x)}{f(x)} \, dx =$	
Complete the probability rule $P(A \cup B) =$	

Quiz R4: Revision 4

A body is trying to slide down an inclined plane. In what direction is the force of friction acting?	
What is the formula for the general term of an arithmetic sequence?	
How is the graph of $f^{-1}(x)$ related to the graph of $f(x)$?	
For small θ, state the small-angle approximations for $\sin(\theta)$ and $\cos(\theta)$	
For the quadratic $ax^2 + bx + c$, if $b^2 - 4ac > 0$ then...	
How do you find the vertical and horizontal components of a force?	
$\int \dfrac{f'(x)}{f(x)} \, dx =$	
Complete the probability rule $P(A \cup B) =$	
$36x^2 - 49$ is an example of...	
What are the four conditions for a binomial distribution to be a valid model of a situation?	
How do you determine if a stationary point of a function is a minimum?	
Sketch the graphs $y = \sin(x)$ and $y = \sin(3x)$	

Quiz R5: Revision 5

ANSWER KEY

R5.1	For what range is the expansion $(a + bx)^n$ valid for negative n?	$\left|\dfrac{bx}{a}\right| < 1 \Rightarrow |x| < \left|\dfrac{a}{b}\right|$
R5.2	Which technique of integration would you use to integrate $\int \sin(x)(x+2)^2 \, dx$?	Integration by parts
R5.3	State the chain rule for differentiation	If $y = f(u)$ and $u = g(x)$ then $\dfrac{dy}{dx} = \dfrac{dy}{du}\dfrac{du}{dx}$
R5.4	How would you solve the differential equation $\dfrac{dy}{dx} = f(x)g(y)$?	Separate the variables and integrate
R5.5	Find (by implicit differentiation) $\dfrac{dy}{dx}$ for the equation $2x^2 y = 4x$	$\dfrac{dy}{dx} = \dfrac{4 - 4xy}{2x^2}$
R5.6	$\dfrac{d}{dx}\sin(x) =$	$\cos(x)$
R5.7	The number of bacteria on the surface of some bread is increasing at a rate directly proportional to the number of bacteria, b, at a given time. Express this as a differential equation	$\dfrac{db}{dt} = kb$
R5.8	How is the gradient of a tangent to a curve at a given point, P, related to the gradient of the normal at the point P?	They are negative reciprocals of each other
R5.9	Define the term "limiting friction"	The friction when friction is at a maximum. $F = \mu R$
R5.10	State Newton's Second Law of Motion	The resultant force is equal to the mass times the acceleration. The force and acceleration act in the same direction
R5.11	Define the term "quota sampling"	A population is divided into categories. Each category is then given a quota of people to sample from. Sampling then continues until all quotas are met
R5.12	For a continuous random variable, X, what is $P(X = c)$ where c is in the domain of the distribution?	0

Quiz R5: Revision 5

TRACKER

Quiz	Date	Score
1		
2		
3		
4		
5		
6		

Got it? ☐

Quiz R5: Revision 5

R5.1	For what range is the expansion $(a + bx)^n$ valid for negative n?	
R5.2	Which technique of integration would you use to integrate $\int \sin(x)(x + 2)^2 \, dx$?	
R5.3	State the chain rule for differentiation	
R5.4	How would you solve the differential equation $\frac{dy}{dx} = f(x)g(y)$?	
R5.5	Find (by implicit differentiation) $\frac{dy}{dx}$ for the equation $2x^2y = 4x$	
R5.6	$\frac{d}{dx} \sin(x) =$	
R5.7	The number of bacteria on the surface of some bread is increasing at a rate directly proportional to the number of bacteria, b, at a given time. Express this as a differential equation	
R5.8	How is the gradient of a tangent to a curve at a given point, P, related to the gradient of the normal at the point P?	
R5.9	Define the term "limiting friction"	
R5.10	State Newton's Second Law of Motion	
R5.11	Define the term "quota sampling"	
R5.12	For a continuous random variable, X, what is $P(X = c)$ where c is in the domain of the distribution?	

Quiz R5: Revision 5

State the chain rule for differentiation	
$\frac{d}{dx}\sin(x) =$	
Define the term "limiting friction"	
For a continuous random variable, X, what is $P(X = c)$ where c is in the domain of the distribution?	
Which technique of integration would you use to integrate $\int \sin(x)(x+2)^2 \, dx$?	
How would you solve the differential equation $\frac{dy}{dx} = f(x)g(y)$?	
How is the gradient of a tangent to a curve at a given point, P, related to the gradient of the normal at the point P?	
State Newton's Second Law of Motion	
For what range is the expansion $(a + bx)^n$ valid for negative n?	
Find (by implicit differentiation) $\frac{dy}{dx}$ for the equation $2x^2 y = 4x$	
The number of bacteria on the surface of some bread is increasing at a rate directly proportional to the number of bacteria, b, at a given time. Express this as a differential equation	
Define the term "quota sampling"	

Quiz R5: Revision 5

State Newton's Second Law of Motion	
For what range is the expansion $(a + bx)^n$ valid for negative n?	
Find (by implicit differentiation) $\dfrac{dy}{dx}$ for the equation $2x^2y = 4x$	
$\dfrac{d}{dx} \sin(x) =$	
Which technique of integration would you use to integrate $\displaystyle\int \sin(x)(x + 2)^2 \, dx$?	
Define the term "limiting friction"	
The number of bacteria on the surface of some bread is increasing at a rate directly proportional to the number of bacteria, b, at a given time. Express this as a differential equation	
Define the term "quota sampling"	
How is the gradient of a tangent to a curve at a given point, P, related to the gradient of the normal at the point P?	
For a continuous random variable, X, what is $P(X = c)$ where c is in the domain of the distribution?	
State the chain rule for differentiation	
How would you solve the differential equation $\dfrac{dy}{dx} = f(x)g(y)$?	

Quiz R5: Revision 5

$\frac{d}{dx}\sin(x) =$	
For a continuous random variable, X, what is $P(X = c)$ where c is in the domain of the distribution?	
For what range is the expansion $(a + bx)^n$ valid for negative n?	
State the chain rule for differentiation	
The number of bacteria on the surface of some bread is increasing at a rate directly proportional to the number of bacteria, b, at a given time. Express this as a differential equation	
Find (by implicit differentiation) $\frac{dy}{dx}$ for the equation $2x^2y = 4x$	
Define the term "quota sampling"	
How is the gradient of a tangent to a curve at a given point, P, related to the gradient of the normal at the point P?	
How would you solve the differential equation $\frac{dy}{dx} = f(x)g(y)$?	
State Newton's Second Law of Motion	
Which technique of integration would you use to integrate $\int \sin(x)(x + 2)^2\, dx$?	
Define the term "limiting friction"	

Quiz R5: Revision 5

State the chain rule for differentiation	
$\dfrac{d}{dx} \sin(x) =$	
Define the term "limiting friction"	
For a continuous random variable, X, what is $P(X = c)$ where c is in the domain of the distribution?	
Which technique of integration would you use to integrate $\displaystyle\int \sin(x)(x + 2)^2 \, dx$?	
How would you solve the differential equation $\dfrac{dy}{dx} = f(x)g(y)$?	
How is the gradient of a tangent to a curve at a given point, P, related to the gradient of the normal at the point P?	
State Newton's Second Law of Motion	
For what range is the expansion $(a + bx)^n$ valid for negative n?	
Find (by implicit differentiation) $\dfrac{dy}{dx}$ for the equation $2x^2y = 4x$	
The number of bacteria on the surface of some bread is increasing at a rate directly proportional to the number of bacteria, b, at a given time. Express this as a differential equation	
Define the term "quota sampling"	

Quiz R5: Revision 5

State Newton's Second Law of Motion	
For what range is the expansion $(a + bx)^n$ valid for negative n?	
Find (by implicit differentiation) $\dfrac{dy}{dx}$ for the equation $2x^2y = 4x$	
$\dfrac{d}{dx}\sin(x) =$	
Which technique of integration would you use to integrate $\int \sin(x)(x+2)^2 \, dx$?	
Define the term "limiting friction"	
The number of bacteria on the surface of some bread is increasing at a rate directly proportional to the number of bacteria, b, at a given time. Express this as a differential equation	
Define the term "quota sampling"	
How is the gradient of a tangent to a curve at a given point, P, related to the gradient of the normal at the point P?	
For a continuous random variable, X, what is $P(X = c)$ where c is in the domain of the distribution?	
State the chain rule for differentiation	
How would you solve the differential equation $\dfrac{dy}{dx} = f(x)g(y)$?	